CONSTITUTIONAL LIFE AND EUROPE'S AREA OF FREEDOM, SECURITY AND JUSTICE

Constitutional Life and Europe's Area of Freedom, Security and Justice

ALUN HOWARD GIBBS
University of Southampton, UK

Routledge
Taylor & Francis Group
LONDON AND NEW YORK

First published 2011 by Ashgate Publishing

2 Park Square, Milton Park, Abingdon, Oxon OX14 4RN
711 Third Avenue, New York, NY 10017, USA

Routledge is an imprint of the Taylor & Francis Group, an informa business

First issued in paperback 2016

British Library Cataloguing in Publication Data
Gibbs, Alun Howard.
Constitutional life and Europe's area of freedom, security and justice. -- (Applied legal philosophy)
1. National security--European Union countries.
2. Justice, Administration of--European Union countries.
3. Civil rights--European Union countries.
4. Constitutional law--European Union countries. 5. Law--European Union countries--International unification.
6. Common good.
I. Title II. Series
342.2'4-dc22

Library of Congress Cataloging-in-Publication Data
Gibbs, Alun Howard.
Constitutional life and Europe's area of freedom, security and justice / by Alun Howard Gibbs.
p. cm. -- (Applied legal philosophy)
Includes bibliographical references and index.
ISBN 978-1-4094-0269-5 (hardback)
1. Internal security--European Union countries. 2. Freedom of movement--European Union countries. 3. Criminal justice, Administration of--European Union countries. 4. International and municipal law--European Union countries. I. Title.
KJE5250.G53 2011
342.24--dc22

2011015827

ISBN 978-1-4094-0269-5 (hbk)
ISBN 978-1-138-25676-7 (pbk)

Contents

Series Editor's Preface

The objective of the Applied Legal Philosophy series is to publish work which adopts a theoretical approach to the study of particular areas or aspects of law or deals with general theories of law in a way which focused on issues of practical moral and political concern in specific legal contexts.

In recent years there has been an encouraging tendency for legal philosophers to utilize detailed knowledge of the substance and practicalities of law and a noteworthy development in the theoretical sophistication of much legal research. The series seeks to encourage these trends and to make available studies in law which are both genuinely philosophical in approach and at the same time based on appropriate legal knowledge and directed towards issues in the criticism and reform of actual laws and legal systems.

The series will include studies of all the main areas of law, presented in a manner which relates to the concerns of specialist legal academics and practitioners. Each book makes an original contribution to an area of legal study while being comprehensible to those engaged in a wide variety of disciplines. Their legal content is principally Anglo-American, but a wide-ranging comparative approach is encouraged and authors are drawn from a variety of jurisdictions.

Tom Campbell
Series Editor
Centre for Applied Philosophy and Public Ethics
Charles Sturt University, Canberra.

Preface

The origins of this book lie in research undertaken at the European Institute, in Florence. I arrived in Florence immediately following the French and Dutch referenda when the populace of these founding countries of the Treaty of Rome voted against ratification of the Constitutional Treaty. Up until this point it had seemed that the Constitutional Treaty would be the foundation stone for a new European Union, in which the political controversies over its democratic pedigree, which had been over-shadowing discussion over increased integration after the Treaty of Maastricht, could be laid to rest. The rejection of the Constitutional Treaty seemed to provoke a complete reassessment concerning the appropriate place of constitutionalism and constitutional theory within our understanding of Europe and European integration. This led to an increasing sense of unease, both in political and academic circles, about whether advancing a theoretical account of Europe in constitutional terms could lead back to a conventional form of constitutionalism in which the relationship between the Union and its constituent Member States is characterised by a formal, hierarchical and monistic account. My own approach to the questions and difficulties of European constitutionalism came via a different route and perspective. Rather than the point of entry being how to conceive, or conceptualise, the relationship between different legal orders as a means of attempting to grapple with what makes the European project coherent despite its clear diversity and plurality, my own research began with the experiences, practices and problems of a specific and highly important aspect of European integration – namely, internal security policy. Therefore, constitutionalism emerged as a way of thinking about the meaning of the integration which was taking place and which formed the basis of a common, European, political activity. I did not approach constitutionalism, or constitutional theory, with a sense that it had a prior and rigid set of meanings or conventions. In this way the book has attempted to contribute to the way we understand a specific area of European integration but in so doing also to bring to light crucial possibilities for the study of constitutionalism.

The principal consideration is to understand the area of freedom, security and justice, in constitutional terms, by pointing to the need to reflect upon common commitments to a political way of life which can sustain the practices of integration. I do not intend to offer a prescriptive sense as to the appropriate limits of integration on internal security policy but rather to indicate that what is taking place must be accompanied by serious constitutional consideration as to what become the dimensions of a common constitutional life. It may be that this does place limitations on integration but it was not my intention to start from such a premise, instead I wanted to encourage a genuine engagement with constitutional thinking about the area of freedom, security and justice as forming part of how the EU is understood as a political community.

This approach to understanding the practices of integration in the area of freedom, security and justice reveals elements of my commitment towards constitutional understanding more generally. The dominant approach to constitutionalism is one in which questions of legitimacy rest upon the rationality of the restraint of sovereign power, by the constituted legal order, and also the converse form in which primary political authority becomes the symbolic power which induces, or compels, a 'we feeling' of compliance and adherence. In each instance constitutionalism rationalises power and compliance within the political order in order to make a claim about the legitimacy of that order. I have attempted to explore a different possibility of thinking through the problem of constitutional legitimacy, and its relationship with 'authority' and 'identity', which emphasises that relational ways of living in political community must be approached as first and foremost practical involvements in the common commitments of a political community and enfolded to us over time. Such an attempt to draw near to what is most essential about the *being with* of political community cannot be driven by the notion that constitutionalism must *master* the question of authority and identity. Such mastery, or at least the very gesture towards mastery, can be most clearly discerned by the desire to search for representations of 'authority' and 'identifications' within the institutions and procedures of the political. The task of thinking through what kind of calling is in constitutional thinking entails abandoning this gesture towards the mastery of the fundamental terms of 'authority' and 'identity'. Instead, constitutional thinking about authority and fundamental belonging become intrinsic, and situational, elements of the common constitutional life. In short, constitutional thinking is concerned with exploring the possibilities of authentic relational ways of living and crucial in this respect, particularly for the European Union, is that it does not seek to arbitrarily fix such an effort through the appeal to the concept of the 'state' or even the 'post state'. We must proceed with care and attentiveness in the task of exploring the meaning, and indeed the strangeness, of the constitutional practices themselves.

Finally, I would like to offer some guidance to the reader concerning the text itself. The Treaty of Lisbon, which came into force during the writing of this book, creates crucial reforms to European Union law, in general, and the area of freedom, security and justice in particular. This book is not intended to be an up-to-date doctrinal account of the law in this area – rather it is written as an interpretation of the constitutional implications of the development of an area of freedom, security and justice as part of our integration towards understanding the European Union as a common political way of life. To this extent the book does not undertake to consider directly the constitutional implications of the Lisbon Treaty on the area of freedom, security and justice even if I have attempted to reflect upon the most recent legal developments. In addition, I considered that it was important to preserve, when discussing the pre-Lisbon law, the old terminology or numbering as this gives a sense of the overall historical development of the AFSJ.

Acknowledgements

I am grateful to members of the European University Institute, where many of the insights of this book were hatched, for creating the most superb environment for research and contemplation. Neil Walker, Kimmo Nuotio and Hans Lindahl provided encouragement in publishing and offered many thought-provoking comments on the original manuscript. At Southampton University I am grateful to Oren Ben Dor for reading and commenting on an earlier draft of Chapter 2 and to the Head of School, Natalie Lee, for creating a pleasant environment to write and teach. I would particularly like to thank Nathan Gibbs for reading the entire manuscript, providing corrections and offering insightful comments. I am grateful for the patient support of Ashgate Publishing. Finally, I would like to acknowledge the grant and scholarship provided by the government of the United Kingdom which supported the original research upon which this book is based.

My personal gratitude is for the loving support of my family and Cláudia Rath.

Alun Howard Gibbs
Southampton University, 2011

Introduction

In 1997, at the signing of the Amsterdam Treaty, it would have taken a particularly far-sighted policy maker to have envisaged quite how significant the new 'area of freedom, security and justice' (AFSJ) would become for European integration in the coming decade. At the inception of the AFSJ internal security measures appear, at first glance, to be a classical instance of a form of functional 'spill-over' from the integration of the internal market; in particular, the objective of freedom of movement and the open internal borders of the Schengen area.[1] However, over the next decade internal security acquired a crucial autonomy from simply being thought of as an adjunct to the internal market-related concerns of fetters to the free movement of persons and the eradication of internal border controls. For example, the Stockholm Programme, published by the Commission of the European Union in December 2009, outlines the policy commitments of the AFSJ from 2010 to 2014, and it illustrates the ambitious long-term policy plans for the AFSJ. Readers of this document can be under no doubt that the AFSJ has developed in such a way as to go beyond a notion of integration 'spill-over' from other, specifically internal market, sectors but rather has emerged as policy area sufficiently successfully to pose a fundamental question about the place of internal security in our understanding of the political union of the EU.

One common way of approaching the question of the emerging autonomy of internal security as part of the political integration taking place at the European level is to refer to the significant events of history as an explanation. The terrorist attacks on 11 September 2001 undoubtedly altered the perception of global risks and threats amongst policy makers, particularly for the allies of America in Europe. Two terrorist attacks in Europe, Madrid (2004) and London (2005), brought to the attention of European policy makers the importance of security provision and the significance of an institutional structure of cooperation and resource sharing in the AFSJ. The connections between internal security integration, in the European Union (EU), and the nature of the current concerns over threats emanating from outside, or inside, the EU are considered to be a legitimate way to understand the trajectory of the AFSJ over the last decade.

Even so, to view the political significance of the AFSJ simply as a consequence of responding to security events, and even its success in so doing, would be to miss a fundamental aspect of its importance as part of the wider political development of

1 A connection which can be illustrated by the fact that the AFSJ actually composed two legal regimes: the first pillar with responsibility for borders and migration and the third pillar with competence in criminal justice, police and judicial co-operation.

the EU. Part of the way to understand this relationship would be to appreciate that as well as being a common market the EU also increasingly understands itself to be a common 'area of freedom, security and justice', or, as Neil Walker succinctly remarks, the AFSJ has become part of the 'polity building' exercise of the EU.[2] This link between the AFSJ and the understanding of the EU as a distinctive political activity, existing alongside those of the state, becomes the principal issue for this book to address as it seems to locate precisely the way in which we might begin to think about the AFSJ in constitutional terms. We might phrase this question in the following terms: how does designating an area of freedom, security and justice become bound up in the deeper issues over the status of the EU as a 'polity'? As I have intimated, this question calls for a different kind of thinking; namely, it calls for a consideration of the AFSJ in constitutional terms.

However, this question masks a much deeper and more significant problem. The question presupposes that the answer to the question lies ready to hand to use or employ within some kind of pre-existing idea about constitutions, perhaps, the stock of knowledge that we call constitutional theory. But the relationship may not be as simple as this. What if the attempt to uncover the relationship between the commitments to an area freedom, security and justice and the understanding of the EU as a political community entails in addition an exploration of the scope of thinking that conventionally we term 'constitutional'? In such circumstances not only must our inquiry be to consider a crucial aspect of EU integration, as important as this is, but, in addition, this task prompts us to explore the possibilities of thinking in constitutional terms itself. Hence, the relationship between the AFSJ and the notion of 'polity building' in the EU manifests itself as a fundamental connection between a consideration of the practices of the AFSJ and the scope of constitutional thinking, with both playing a role in advancing the paths of the other.

As a way of introducing the main argument, before outlining in more detail how this appears in the different chapters, I would like to indicate how the term 'constitution' is developed in the course of the book. It is apparent that the word 'constitution' is found in a family of words – for example, 'constitutional' and 'constitutionalism' – which broadly aim to refer to the practices related, or connected, to the constitution of a political community. As I have already indicated, what emerges as a particular concern are those practices of the AFSJ which indicate the relationship to the understanding of the EU as a political community – it is in this sense that I will be employing the term 'constitutional'. The broader claim that I make, in this respect, is that constitutionalism, as a form of study and scholarship, entails the challenge to consider anew relational ways of living as a political community rather than seeking a stable, or fixed, definition of constitutionalism. It is this mode of thinking that lies behind that part of the title of the book, 'constitutional life'.

2 Neil Walker, 'In Search of the Area of Freedom, Security and Justice: A Constitutional Odyssey', in *Europe's Area of Freedom, Security and Justice*, edited by Neil Walker (Oxford: Oxford University Press, 2004), p. 11.

Considering the scope of possibilities of thinking about 'constitutional life', which is prompted by the practices of the area of freedom, security and justice, becomes the challenge of addressing and conveying constitutional concerns beyond those conventionally used in constitutional theory. Bound up with the effort to consider 'constitutional life' is the challenge to preserve the *distinctiveness* of thinking about political community and the relationship to constitutional authority. In this way I do not propose, or set out to critique, oppose or defeat conventional ways of thinking about constitutions as such efforts of deliberate critical thinking often end in superficiality, or worse still, maintaining the status quo one has sought to oppose. If the account of constitutional thinking does reveal the limitations or difficulties of conventional constitutional thinking it does so not through a deliberate act of opposition, but rather by the necessity of thinking through the difficulties that we confront in our encounter with the practices of the AFSJ, and the EU.

In order to look at the ways in which freedom, security and justice relate to our understanding of the EU as a political community we need to establish a meaningful distinction between constitutionalism and the intention of policy makers to meet the demands that the EU is to be at the forefront of measures to ensure that individual interests concerning security can be met, and balanced, with measures designed to promote freedom and justice. In other words, in this book I attempt to distinguish between a constitutional claim to represent freedom, security and justice and an understanding which sees these goods to be instrumentally provided or delivered in terms of substantive measures or policy.

Part of the task of thinking about constitutionalism, in such a way as to preserve its distinctiveness, is to deepen and explore the language of constitutionalism. In the course of this book I often refer to 'constitutional life' as being part of the 'common commitments of a political way of life over time' or of advocating a form of constitutionalism which entails an 'ontological turn'. I will consider what I mean by these terms and descriptions throughout the book, and particularly in Chapter 2, but broadly they form part of the overall trajectory of this effort towards thinking about the constitutional as a mode of involvement or participation in a practice in such a way as to reveal the way we understand ourselves as committed to a constitutional way of life, including those practices related to the AFSJ.

Having briefly considered the approach of this book towards the idea of carrying out a constitutional study of the AFSJ I would like to introduce the themes taken up by the different chapters and how the overall argument of the book is developed in each chapter. Chapter 1 explores the practices and developmental history of the AFSJ as part of the wider understanding of the EU as a political community or polity. The articulation that the EU constitutes an area of freedom, security and justice becomes intimately bound up not only with the attempts to deepen integration at the European level but also with concerns about the constitutional legitimacy of such practices. This apparent paradox between the depth of integration, which presupposes a common political way of life in the EU, and the concerns about how to understand such a political community beyond the state becomes the concern over the constitutional legitimacy of that which is taking place.

The issue over how to understand what we might mean by constitutional legitimacy in such a way as not to presuppose any particular form, or structure, of political community becomes the focus of Chapter 2. In this chapter constitutional legitimacy is interpreted to mean the common commitments of a political community over time whereby notions of 'authority' and 'identification' are not means of inducing or compelling compliance with a constituted order, or indeed products of it, but instead become ways of relating and transforming our common commitments to a political way of life. This chapter draws on hermeneutics, particularly the deep interpretative approach of Hans-Georg Gadamer, in order to show how different relational ways of living require us to become interpreters of our common commitments so as to be able to acknowledge how they are enfolded to us over time and are inherently valuable, as opposed to realising particular or delivering specified needs.

Chapter 3 extends this work by suggesting that the representation of freedom, security and justice, as the public goods of the EU, must be considered as constitutional commitments – or as I also write, 'constitutional public goods'. The aim of this chapter is to highlight the distinction between an instrumental and a constitutional way of understanding public goods. The purpose behind this chapter is to suggest that questions of constitutional legitimacy cannot be explored if we only consider freedom, security and justice to be instrumental public goods and fail to consider how they can form part of the constitutional commitments of the EU.

The potential problems of assuming public goods to be instrumental rather than as having the capacity to become the constitutional commitments of a political way of life are developed further in Chapter 4 when I consider the specific example of security as a constitutional public good. It is in this chapter that we begin to encounter the unique difficulties facing the AFSJ as furthering a political and constitutional understanding of the EU more generally. It is argued that security seems to provide the most apparent sense of constitutional legitimacy for the practices of the AFSJ whilst paradoxically tending towards an instrumentality which covers over or conceals its own constitutional pedigree and crucially the call for constitutional thinking. I explore these aspects of security by drawing on the work of Michel Foucault, in particular, his notion of 'governmentality'. I argue that placing limits, or restraining, such practices entails reinvigorating a common language which can allow us to express and interpret common constitutional commitments in a non-instrumental way, including the good of 'security', and that by doing so we can reconcile ourselves as to the limitations of instrumental modes of understanding public goods and the dependency on constitutional life.

The last two substantive chapters of the book, Chapters 5 and 6, mark something of a shift in emphasis towards exploring the actual practices of the AFSJ in terms of how free movement of persons is evoked as part of a common *area* of freedom, security and justice (Chapter 5), and also how criminal law asserts a common *area* of justice to the European Union. In both instances it is acknowledged that the practices of the AFSJ must be grounded on the commitment to a constitutional life if the AFSJ is to be part of way we think about the EU as a legitimate political community. However, both in studies of a common area of justice and in the practices of free movement it is apparent that the approach taken is that constitutional legitimacy can be established not through thinking about constitutional life but rather about perfecting the procedures of the instrumental delivery of goods and, in particular, the instrumental good of security. Finally, in Chapter 7, there are concluding reflections on what the notion of constitutional life might hold for us in the way we think about the site of justice of a political community. The chapter considers what might lie behind the message of hermeneutics and the call to learning that it evokes.

Chapter 1
Constitutional Life and the Area of Freedom, Security and Justice

Introduction: Why a Constitutional Account?

The task which has been undertaken is to begin to understand why constitutional thinking becomes an appropriate lens to bring to awareness the European Union's policy developments in the area of freedom, security and justice. Embarking on such a line of enquiry is not confined to positing justifications for 'using' constitutionalism in a policy field which lacks, in some important senses, the strong 'supranational' components of policy making which are to be found in the internal market domain. And neither can our constitutional analysis set itself the goal of presuming to identify, or confirm, a normative framework for the continued expansion, and primacy, of EU legal norms on internal security. In turning towards constitutional thinking, to explore the implications of the AFSJ, the task becomes a more subtle one than we might immediately assume since the difficulty, and the challenge to constitutionalism, is in being able to reveal how the AFSJ brings to light certain aspects of constitutionalism that have been neglected, or that have not been at the forefront of our concerns. It is this requirement to embark upon an exploration as to what is going on in the AFSJ which will help us to draw near to a way of uncovering what is most essential about constitutionalism. It is this close inter-connection between constitutional thinking and the requirement to consider the practices of the AFSJ that becomes the important path for this book to take. Therefore, the success of this task will be to what extent it enables the developments of the AFSJ to prompt us to question our presuppositions about what constitutional thinking *is*.

In order to attempt to locate a means of exploring this more challenging relationship between constitutional theory and the AFSJ it is worthwhile to begin by examining the principal reasons for a shift in which a constitutional understanding of the AFSJ becomes plausible in the first place. At this stage the analysis will be confined to introductory remarks preparing the way for a more detailed scrutiny of these developments later in the chapter. Each of the three headings below set out the development of the AFSJ in terms of: (i) policy, (ii) institutions and (iii) critical commentary. The intention is to introduce the practices and developmental stages of the AFSJ in such a way as to demonstrate the relationship between the AFSJ and its wider connection with the wider political integration of the EU.

Policy Expansion

This justification cites the continued growth and centrality of internal security as a policy goal since the Member States first began to cooperate with one another on such matters over 30 years ago. The earliest cooperation became known as 'Trevi' and from the outset such meetings were envisaged to be a flexible and highly specialised form of technical cooperation, on a purely inter-governmental basis.[1] Certainly the genesis of Trevi seems to be as a direct consequence of the increasing level of violence and organised criminality in Europe during the early 1970s, which had also taken on a transnational character. It was understood that these emerging and complex international crime networks required a more sophisticated and coordinated response by states and other policing and law-enforcement agencies.[2] The kind of subject matter under consideration within the Trevi structure entirely reflected the emerging security concerns of the participating states and the expertise that the specialist agencies felt able to share with each other. The emerging policies can be understood as falling under the following subject areas: the assessments of terrorist threats to important civil resources such as aircraft and power stations; the coordination of policing matters, for instance, tactics, training and information regarding the deployment of certain specialist equipment; and finally cooperation over technical matters in other areas of serious organised crime, such as drug-trafficking, arms smuggling and large-scale bank robberies.

Over the next 30 years the dimensions of these policy areas expanded to include the vital matters of asylum, immigration and border control. At such a point it could be considered that the policy had arisen from the spill-over of measures required to augment the internal market. However, there was increasing penetration of these policy objectives into the national sphere which has led to both an enhanced awareness of the significance of the AFSJ in national politics and that these measures have become distinct from the efforts to complete the internal market.[3] For instance, by the early 2000s the European Union had ambitious plans for the common development of criminal justice systems, including the mutual recognition of judicial decisions, which took legislative shape with the European Arrest Warrant (EAW)[4] providing a shared scheme for the extradition of suspects

1 Although Trevi started with a meeting, in Rome, of the Ministers of Justice Home Affairs from each of the Members of the EC, the co-operation did not take place within the institutional form of the EC.

2 See Anderson et al., *Policing in the European Union* (Oxford: Clarendon Press, 1995), p. 24.

3 Neil Walker, 'In Search of the Area of Freedom, Security and Justice: A Constitutional Odyssey', in *Europe's Area of Freedom, Security and Justice* edited by Neil Walker (Oxford: Oxford University Press, 2004) at p. 16.

4 2002/584/JHA: 'Council Framework Decision of 13 June 2002 on the European Arrest Warrant and the surrender procedures', OJ L190 (18 July 2002), pp. 1–20.

between Member States.[5] In recent years it has become clear that a paramount reason why internal security has acquired the policy dynamism that has resulted in the ambitious and extensive proposals apparent, particularly with the Hague, and most recently the Stockholm Programme, is '9/11'.[6] The alteration of global security, perceived or actual, following the unprecedented nature of the terrorist attacks, gave the EU a united and common interest to pursue and strengthen measures relating to internal security. The policy area which was organised, by the Treaty of Amsterdam, into the 'area of freedom, security and justice', in 1997, has subsequently acquired a clear sense of its purpose and the importance of its place in developing the wider dimensions of political integration.

Institutional Developments

Policy expansion has gone hand-in-hand with institutional developments over the course of the same period of time. As outlined above, cooperation began at an inter-governmental level in Trevi and, although there was a measure of institutional organisation through the various specialist Working Groups, the organisation of policy took place on the flexible and informal basis of soft-law recommendations, opinions and declarations. However, the narrative of institutional development is one of a gradual but definite shift from the purely inter-governmental to the supranational; where the institutional organisation of justice and home affairs gradually reflects the increased significance of the collective EU institutions in the development of policy.

The Maastricht Treaty (1992) saw the creation of the third pillar, which was called 'Cooperation in the Fields of Justice and Home Affairs'. The provisions of the third pillar were not part of the three Treaties establishing the European Communities and, therefore, were not part of European Community law; in consequence, the general legal acts of the EC – regulations, directives and decisions – were not applicable to the third pillar. In fact, the most formal legal instrument available to Member States was still the multilateral Treaty, or Convention, which would be governed by the principles of public international law, although there was also the possibility of employing the declaration of 'joint positions'. The entire tenor of the approach taken in transposing Trevi to the EU seems to have been an attempt to preserve the inter-governmental character of the cooperation already developed in Trevi. This is further evidenced by the fact that the roles of

5 The European Arrest Warrant also applies to the execution of custodial sentences between Member States.

6 Communication from the Commission to the European Council and Parliament of 10 May 2005, 'The Hague Programme: Ten priorities for the next five years – the partnership for European renewal in the field of Freedom, Security and Justice', COM (2005) 184. Also, see the joint statement by the Council and the Commission on the Action Plan for the implementation of the Hague Programme, OJ L198 (12.8.2005), pp. 1–22. European Commission: 'Action Plan Implementing the Stockholm Programme', COM (2010)171.

the main EC institutions – Parliament, Commission and European Court of Justice – were heavily circumscribed. The Commission was not granted exclusive right to initiate measures, which it enjoyed in the first pillar; instead, it was to share this privilege with the Member States. Furthermore, it was emphasised that matters relating to internal security, law and order were to remain the exclusive domain of the Member States.[7] The European Parliament (EP) was given a modicum of scrutiny powers under the co-decision procedure as it was required to be consulted and informed on a regular basis about the various activities of the third pillar and was also able to ask questions and make recommendations to the Council or Commission.[8] However, in reality, the scrutiny provided by the EP was *ex post facto* regarding the legislative process, that is to say, it was not involved in the development of third pillar measures. The role of the ECJ was also severely limited, no doubt as a consequence of the significance of ECJ jurisprudence in the early development of the EC. The ECJ could only hear a case concerning a Member State about a third pillar matter if that Member State had first consented to this.[9] The institutional motor of the third pillar, during the Maastricht era, was the Council and the co-ordinating committee, K4, named after the article in the Treaty that established it. Composed of the Member States, it was in the Council that the principal policy goals were formulated. Desirous of preserving an inter-governmental character to the running of the third pillar, unanimity was required amongst the Member States for a measure to be agreed and also the ultimate right of initiative resided with the Council. The K4 committee preserved much of the technical apparatus developed under the Trevi regime, including the use of Working Groups to harness a range of expertise to tackle the policy areas of JHA.[10]

In 1997 the Treaty of Amsterdam offered an opportunity to reassess the achievements of the JHA pillar. In the period since TEU there had been increasing awareness, primarily by policy makers at the European level, of deficiencies concerning the institutional framework of the third pillar.[11] The legal framework appeared inadequate to support and effectively deliver the policy goals of the

7 Article K.2 TEU(M); 'This Title shall not affect the exercise of the responsibilities incumbent upon Member States with regard to the maintenance of law and order and the safeguarding of internal security'.

8 Article K.6 TEU.

9 Article K.3 TEU.

10 Monica den Boer notes that a complex relationship developed between the working parties and experts of the K4 Committee and COREPER, the main administrative centre in the EU structure. This leads den Boer to describe the procedure as involving 'a circus of actors, who compete for policy space, forms a perfect breeding ground for rivalry and friction. The tensions between the swift-acting COREPER and the loose congregation of individuals in the K4 Committee have become legendary'. See Monica den Boer, 'Europe and the Art of International Police Co-operation: Free Fall or Measured Scenario?' in O'Keeffe and Twomey (eds), at p. 306.

11 See, in particular, the article by David O'Keeffe, 'Reforming the Third Pillar: Transparency and Structural Reform in the Long-Term Perspective', in *Justice and Home*

third pillar. There were also concerns relating to the practical operations of the different Working and Steering Groups.[12] A consensus was emerging that favoured reform of decision-making, the introduction of new objectives, legal instruments and improved judicial control. Despite this consensus on the substantive need for reform it was not agreed whether this would be better achieved by full or partial 'communitarisation', or some other alternative.[13] The result was that the third pillar was split with visas, borders, immigration, asylum and civil law being transferred to the first pillar, and a five-year transition period was instigated (ending 1 May 2004), following which these matters would be dealt with according to the EC legislative method.[14] This meant that the third pillar was reduced to judicial and police cooperation and criminal justice, as well as incorporating new responsibilities for measures designed to combat racism and xenophobia. However, having split the policies of the old Maastricht JHA into two legislative methods, first and third pillar, the EU sought to unify internal security under a broad policy heading. Article 29 (under the old numbering) states:

> Without prejudice to the powers of the European Community, the Union's objective shall be to provide citizens with a high level of safety within *an area of freedom, security and justice…*[15]

A final aspect of the institutional changes at Amsterdam was the introduction of a legislative procedure for the adoption of measures in the 'third pillar'. Article 34 introduces the 'framework decision' which is intended for 'the approximation of the laws and regulations of the Member States' in a manner that is binding, but leaves to the national authorities the choice of form and methods. On the face of it the framework decision is very similar to the directive (used in the first pillar) because it has legally binding force as to the result to be achieved, but preserves flexibility for the Member State to adapt such measures as it sees fit, and which are coherent within its own legal system. This is where the comparison to a directive ends – since Article 34 explicitly states that the framework decisions cannot bestow legal rights on individuals to be enforced in national courts or tribunals, it lacks direct effect.

Affairs in the EU: The Development of the Third Pillar, edited by Roland Bieber and Jorg Monar (European University Press, Bruges Conference, 1995).

12 Dora Kostakopolou, 'The Area of Freedom, Security and Justice under the New Constitution', *Academy of European Law*, European University Institute, July 2005.

13 Jorg Monar, 'Justice and Home Affairs in the Treaty of Amsterdam: Reform at the Price of Fragmentation', 23 *European Law Review* (1998), pp. 320–335.

14 However, the detail is a little more complex. Following the ending of the transition period it was decided according to Article 67(2) EC to keep unanimity and consultation of the EP in respect of legal migration, family law and asylum issues which were not yet part of the provisions of Article 67(5). See Steve Peers, *Justice and Home Affairs* (Oxford: Oxford University Press, 2006), p. 25.

15 Article 29, Title VI, TEU(M). My emphasis.

The institutional reforms at Amsterdam did not, however, represent a stable settlement since over the following few years the third pillar of the AFSJ was increasingly implicated in debates over the Constitutional Treaty, which envisaged that the 'pillar system' of the Maastricht Treaty would be brought to an end and that the Union would enjoy a common legislative regime. Despite the failure of the Constitutional Treaty, in the summer of 2005, the case for reform of the third pillar continued and plans were drawn up in the Lisbon Treaty (which came into force on 1 December 2009).

The main elements of the changes introduced under the Lisbon Treaty are to extend what was once termed the 'community method' to the AFSJ by abolishing the distinction between Title VI and Title IV that has existed ever since the Maastricht Treaty on European Union. The new regime is expressed in Article 67 of the Treaty on the Functioning of the European Union (TFEU):

> The Union shall constitute an area of freedom, security and justice with respect for fundamental rights and the different legal systems and traditions of the Member States.

Since 2009 there has no longer been a 'third pillar' legal regime as regards police and judicial cooperation in criminal matters. Furthermore, all AFSJ measures are now adopted according to the usual legislative measures (regulations, directives and decisions) and by the 'ordinary legislative procedure' (co-decision and QMV in Council).[16] In addition, the Court of Justice gains full jurisdictional powers of control (including over the agencies of the AFSJ).[17] The AFSJ now has the institutional composition to compliment the far-reaching policy agenda that was outlined in the previous section.

Critical Commentary

Finally, awareness of the increasing significance of internal security, as a policy area for the EU, has burgeoned in recent times and whilst this may not yet have reached the level of interest that the internal market enjoys it now constitutes a significant body of literature. Much of this commentary directly reflects upon the constitutional implications of the policy and institutional developments; for instance, one of the leading collections examining the AFSJ as a policy area is *Europe's Area of Freedom, Security and Justice*, edited by Neil Walker, which offers an overview of the entire policy field. There are also contributions which focus on specific aspects of AFSJ competence, and in particular, criminal law or

---

16 Article 87 Treaty on the Functioning of the European Union (TFEU). However, unanimity is still retained in respect of operational co-operation, Article 86(3) TFEU, and in additional for those measures proposing the harmonisation of crime (Article 83 TFEU).

17 Article 263 TFEU, the exclusion for Member State police operations and the exercise of law and order responsibilities remain.

immigration, visas, borders and asylum matters. Equally, it is apparent that there is a diversity of views as to whether the policy and institutional developments in the AFSJ offer grounds for a constitutional narrative which is capable of providing a robust normative grounding for the AFSJ.[18] Notwithstanding these difficulties most commentators are convinced that the AFSJ does pose crucial constitutional questions, principally because such policy naturally has a profound effect on individual rights and political freedom. As a consequence a great deal of scrutiny is expended upon the political and legal mechanisms, or procedures, of the AFSJ and whether they meet the requisite standards of accountability, transparency and human rights protection. It is, however, apparent that any deeper study of the AFSJ must address why it is possible to make claims about 'accountability' and 'human rights', in other words, our understanding as to how internal security integration forms an integral part of how we see our common way of life in the EU.

Drawing upon each of these three justifications it would seem that there is a convincing case for treating the AFSJ as a policy area which raises constitutional issues and considerations. Nevertheless, satisfying ourselves that it would be fruitful to embark upon a constitutional approach brings to the fore deeper questions than simply an account of the policy, institutional or critical developments. Firstly, it is not clear what kind of standard we are referring to when we use the term 'constitutional', or even whether it can be properly conceived as a 'standard' at all. Does the evocation of the term 'constitutional' only become possible because of the specific type of policy, or policy making? Does the development of internal security always, and inevitably, require a constitutional justification? Or are we using constitutionalism to mean a certain type of legal and political institutional structure for which we might claim there is an organising or primary norm? Finally, might constitutionalism be a standard of democratic representation, or a means of ensuring the equal participation of all whose interests are affected through procedural rights and protection of fundamental freedoms? Perhaps productive constitutional enquiries may involve responses to all, or some, of these considerations but each of these questions relies upon, or rests upon, a deeper question: why does that which is taking place in the AFSJ *concern* us constitutionally? Another way of posing this question is to suggest that it is primarily a concern over the legitimacy of the AFSJ that compels us to employ the term constitutionalism. Taking this as a possible basis for further inquiry the chapter seeks to explore why it is that the AFSJ *concerns* us in such a way as to compel us to explore whether it is constitutionally legitimate.

18 For instance, see: *A Right to Inclusion and Exclusion: Normative Fault-lines of the EU's Area of Freedom, Security and Justice*, edited by Hans Lindahl (Oxford: Hart Publishing, 2009).

The 'Absence of the State' and the Ensuing Crisis of Legitimacy

If we are right to recast the constitutional question for the AFSJ as one which considers what it is that concerns us about the AFSJ then we must look for a way of approaching this issue. To begin with we might cast the net somewhat wider by acknowledging that although the AFSJ does have a distinctive policy and institutional development ultimately it does form an integral part of the European Union (EU). The advantage of trying to locate our concerns over the AFSJ by considering how it relates to the wider understanding of the EU is that, firstly, we benefit from the longer period of time in which an awareness of the emergence of significant practices of integration 'beyond the sovereign state' have been present and, secondly, this provides us with a much richer vein of literature which responds to this issue.

It is by now a familiar and well-rehearsed narrative that the European Court of Justice (ECJ), an institution which is now known under the Lisbon Treaty as the Court of Justice of the European Union, laid down a strong interpretive teleology for the EC Treaty. In the two seminal cases from the early 1960s, *Van Gend en Loos*[19] and *Costa v ENEL*,[20] the ECJ provided the building blocks for the subsequent 'supranational' teleology of the Community (first) pillar. Firstly, the ECJ asserted that the Community legal order enjoys an autonomous sovereignty stemming from the limitation of the Member States' sovereign rights and exhibited in its capacity to override domestic legal provisions. A second, and related, point is that the EC Treaty did not simply establish rights and obligations between States but also provided a direct relationship with the individual, in order to ensure that any person can go before the national court to plead rights bestowed upon him under the Treaty. The twin claims of the supremacy of EC law over the national legal order and its direct effect within the national legal context have proven contentious and controversial but have always featured in subsequent reasoning by the ECJ in important cases.[21]

Nevertheless, what remains highly problematic is the claim that the legal order of the EU is an autonomous legal order, 'a new legal order'; that is to say, its sovereignty is not derivative from the Member States. The question that follows is how might we understand, and justify, this 'supranational' legal order.[22] The

19 Case 26/62 *Van Gend en Loos v Nederlandse Administratie der Belastingen* [1963] ECR 1.

20 Case 6/64 *Costa v ENEL* [1964] ECR 585.

21 See the example of Francovich and state liability – and now featured in the protocol of the Lisbon Treaty.

22 Giovanni Mancini, 'Europe the case for statehood', 4 *European Law Journal* (1998), pp. 43–62 and the corresponding critique by J.H.H. Weiler in the same edition, 'Europe: the Case Against the Case for Statehood', p. 62. Also consult, J.H.H. Weiler and U.R. Haltern, 'The Autonomy of the Community Legal Order – Through the Looking Glass', 37 *Harvard International Law Journal* (1996), pp. 411–448 and P. Craig, 'Constitutions,

uncertain sense that the EU has the potential to represent a wholly new way of thinking about the form of politics and law is well expressed by Larry Siedentop, 'a great constitutional debate need not involve a prior commitment to federalism as the most desirable outcome in Europe. It may reveal that Europe is in the process of inventing a new political form, something more than a confederation but less than a federation – an association of sovereign states…'[23]

The shift towards a political and legal structure which is 'post-national' or 'beyond the state' creates uncertainty because it compels us to reflect upon the legitimate basis, or foundation, of this shift in legal and political form. For instance, the influential social theorist Jürgen Habermas has written that the challenge of the 'post-national constellation', exemplified by the EU, becomes the question as to how we are able to preserve the liberal and democratic achievements of the nation state.[24] What is characteristic about this argument is that the state – and more particularly the history of the nation state in Europe – is seen as being the basis for constructing a normative framework by which to assess the constitutional legitimacy of the EU. The role that the state plays in arguments over the criteria for legitimacy for the EU, as going beyond the state, is highly complex and is exhibited in a number of different positions. I would like to consider three examples of influential positions in current constitutional theory where the issue of the legitimacy of the EU becomes intimately connected with the notion of the 'state', or perhaps more controversially, 'the absence of the state'.

Demos – The Political Peoples

It was the influential decision of the *Bundesverfassungsgericht* (German Constitutional Court) in *Brunner*,[25] which considered whether the Treaty on European Union infringed the rights accorded to German citizens under their Constitution, which thrust the notion of *demos* to the fore of the constitutional theory debates about the legitimacy of the EU. *Demos* is a word derived from the Greek meaning, broadly, 'ordinary people' but in the present-day context we might think of it as referring to 'citizens' or 'political people'. In a famous passage of the *Brunner* decision the *Bundesverfassungsgericht*, the German Constitutional

---

Constitutionalism and the European Union', 7 *European Law Journal*, pp. 125–150, Trevor Hartley, *Constitutional Problems of the European Union* (Oxford: Hart Publishing, 1999), Chapter 7 and Theodor Schilling, 'The Autonomy of the Community Legal Order: An Analysis of Possible Foundations', 37, *Harvard International Law Journal* (1996), pp. 389–409.

23 Larry Siedentop, *Democracy in Europe* (London: Allen Lane, 2000).

24 'the challenge before us is not to invent anything but to conserve the great democratic achievements of the European nation state, beyond its own limits', see Jürgen Habermas, 'Why Europe Needs a Constitution', *New Left Review* 11 (2001), pp. 5–26 at p. 6.

25 *Brunner and Others v The European Union Treaty* [1994] 1 CMLR 57.

Court, linked the notion of a people with constitutional legitimacy in such a way as to draw a conceptual and normative distinction between the state and the EU:

> If the peoples of the individual States provide democratic legitimation through the agency of their national Parliaments (as at present) limits are then set by virtue of the democratic principle to the extension of the European Communities' functions and powers. Each of the Peoples of the individual States is the starting point for a State power relating to that people. The States need sufficiently important spheres of activity of their own in which the people of each can develop and articulate itself in a process of political will-formation which it legitimates and controls, in order thus to give legal expression to what binds the people together (to a greater or lesser degree of homogeneity) spiritually, socially and politically.[26]

The fundamental presupposition of the Court is that the legal and institutional order of the state becomes an agent in the representation of the pre-existing unity of the 'people' – and so legitimacy becomes a question of what originally 'binds a people together' prior to the institutional and legal order of the nation state. Dieter Grimm expands upon this position in his academic writings by suggesting that there is a minimum, and necessary, social integration[27] for there to be legitimate legal and political institutions. It is apparent that the success of this type of argument depends upon us accepting the deductive reasoning which starts from the premise that legitimate political and legal institutions derive this sense of constitutional legitimacy from the pre-existing social and cultural bonds of the 'people' and ends with the conclusion that the EU does not enjoy such legitimacy because it lacks a 'people' sharing deep rooted social and cultural bonds. It is, of course, possible to attack both the premises of this deductive syllogism and its conclusion,[28] but what is noteworthy here is that legitimacy is assumed to have a set of properties or conditions which are inherently located in the nation- state and hence enables comparison with the EU, as non-state. Rather like the way in which we might posit an archetype or ideal-type, so in this example concerning the understanding and meaning of the term *demos* it is the state that performs the role of marking, and demarking, the ultimate justification of political life and serves to indicate that whatever legitimacy, if any, the EU enjoys it is something which is significantly different from the state.

26 Para. 44, p. 88.

27 Grimm provides an indication of the elements of social cohesion: shared language; cultural or religious attitudes, common myths, histories or legends. See Dieter Grimm, 'Integration by Constitution', 3 *I.CON* (2005), pp. 193–208.

28 For instance, see Joseph H.H. Weiler, 'Does Europe Need a Constitution? Reflections on Demos, Telos and the German Maastricht Decision', 1 *European Law Journal* (1995), pp. 219–258.

Public Philosophy and a Civic Culture

Constitutional theorists, and also political figures, have attempted to resolve the uncertainty surrounding the constitutional legitimacy of the EU by attempting to outline what might be the *finalité*, or the end-justifications, of integration. The call to consider the *finalité* of the European Union has been attributed to the speech by the German Foreign Minister Joschka Fischer at the Humboldt University in Berlin.[29] However, the path that led towards seeking a uniform constitutional settlement for the EU cannot be easily reduced entirely to one single speech. The dynamics were present in the long-debated concerns over the democratic foundation of the EU. The Constitutional Treaty borrowed heavily from the symbolism and imagery of the patriotic republican tradition.[30] The narrative concerning the failings of the Constitutional Treaty is familiar and it would not be fruitful to carry out a further post-mortem here; nevertheless, what is of deeper significance is the extent to which the legitimacy crisis of the EU prompted an attempt to explore the possibilities of a 'public philosophy' for the EU. It is this issue that has the potential to prove more resilient than the, almost forgotten, efforts at drafting a documentary constitution.

The changing nature of European integration entailed moving beyond the completion of the internal market (EC) to the wider social and political goals of the EU. This dynamic led to the need to search for political justifications which went further than market freedoms and consumerism in order to sustain, and legitimise, a shift in the pace and character of integration taking place.[31] (I shall comment more on this point in due course, as the AFSJ forms a crucial part of advancing political integration beyond the internal market.) Hence the emergence of a public philosophy concerning the EU rests on providing a normative basis for the continuation and deepening of integration. As Ian Ward has remarked, such an endeavour actually has close affiliations with the concerns of the humanist writers of Europe such as Gottfried Wilhelm Leibniz, who wrote of a European *respublica* consisting of universal benevolence in search of the common good. Also in this vein of enlightened thinkers Kant wrote of the 'cosmopolitan right' in his essay on *Perpetual Peace*.[32] There were, of course, historical antecedents even to the

29 See the speech given by the (now former) German Foreign Minister, Joschka Fischer, 'From Confederacy to Federation: Thoughts on the Finality of European Integration', speech delivered at the Humboldt University, Berlin, 12 May 2000 < http://centers.law.nyu.edu/jeanmonnet/papers/00/joschka_fischer_en.rtf>

30 See Joseph H.H. Weiler, 'Europe's Tragic Choice', *Jean Monnet Working Papers*, 2000.

31 Ulrich Haltern, 'Pathos and Patina: The Failure and Promise of Constitutionalism in the European Imagination', 9 *European Law Journal* (2003), pp. 14–44 and Nathan Gibbs, 'European Constitutionalism, the Temporal Dimension of Juridical Order and Modern Social Imaginary', 21 *Law and Critique* (2010), pp. 147–162.

32 See the discussion that Ian Ward develops in 'Beyond Constitutionalism: The Search for the European Political Imagination', 7 *European Law Journal*, pp. 32–40.

secular claims of European *respublica* in the seventeenth century. Nevertheless, the point that Ward, and others, make is that the search for common humanist values to sustain a common political way of life must be embarked upon if a political Union is to achieve constitutional legitimacy.[33] Inevitably, sketching a normative account of the European public sphere relies upon many of the achievements of the state tradition – a legal and institutional commitment to fundamental rights, welfare protection and a substantive notion of political citizenship.[34] The tendency to draw upon the *finalité* of the state in the public philosophy of the EU enables us to identify, according to this view, the issue of constitutional legitimacy with the normative political values that underpin the nation state[35] which resolves, or limits, the need to reflect further upon constitutionalism. As a consequence, if our normative concerns about constitutional legitimacy can be resolved, or indeed settled by a public philosophy of the EU, the outstanding issue is one of empirical delivery upon defined goals. The assumption that public philosophy, or normative theory, can finally resolve the concerns over constitutional legitimacy has given rise to tensions and scepticisms that I would now like to consider.

Scepticisms and Legitimacy Delivery

That the constitutional tradition of the state has formed an integral part of the legitimacy questions of the EU is a familiar narrative and, indeed, it may not even be wholly surprising, since, like buildings, we must construct our political and legal lives from the materials we have around us. Nevertheless, what is worthy of further exploration is the reaction to the notion that Europe needs a public philosophy if it is to support and sustain continued integration. For it is possible to discern a considerable degree of scepticism, if not pessimism, about the capabilities of constitutionalism to do just this. It can be seen from the *Brunner* decision, mentioned above, that straightforward claims to a single European authority, or supremacy, are essentially contested, and that the very existence of constitutional

33 For further examples of such a view see, Jürgen Habermas, *The Postnational Constellation: Political Essays*, trans. and ed. by Max Pensky (Cambridge, MA: MIT Press, 2001), Neil MacCormick, *Questioning Sovereignty: Law, State and Nation in the European Commonwealth* (Oxford: Oxford University Press, 1999).

34 For a general discussion of these issues see Joseph Weiler, *The Constitution of Europe: Do the New Clothes have a New Emperor?* (Cambridge: Cambridge University Press, 1999). For an investigation of the human rights dimensions of integration see, Armin Von Bogdandy, 'The European Union as a Human Rights Organization? Human Rights at the Core of the European Union', 37 *Common Market Law Review* (2000), pp. 1307–1338.

35 For instance, it is worth considering the work of Mattias Kumm as this resorts to a normative consideration of the 'integrity' of the practice of European law, 'The Jurisprudence of Constitutional Conflict: Constitutional Supremacy in Europe before and after the Constitutional Treaty', 11 *European Law Journal* (2005), pp. 262–307.

authority is one of flux and up for negotiation.[36] Whilst the descriptive reality of the EU, as a plurality of constitutional orders, may have led to scepticism about the manner and form of constitutionalism (as a unity); for instance as to whether, or not, it closely resembles the monistic state, pluralism has not ultimately led to the abandonment of the notion of constitutionalism. The constitutional pluralists have attempted to invest the notion of constitutionalism with an important role in the negotiation of the 'frames' of plurality in the EU. However, it seems unclear the extent to which constitutional pluralism can operate with a strong, or thick, notion of constitutionalism, for fear that this will revert to a further monistic public philosophy for the EU. As a consequence, it appears that a genuinely insightful descriptive account of pluralism sits uneasily with normative understandings of constitutionalism as a form of unified authority.[37]

Even if the acknowledgement of pluralism, in the EU, leads to a scepticism, or even a revision, of our understanding of constitutionalism it is possible to turn political science literature to encounter more fundamental grounds for doubting whether public philosophy can provide the basis for exploring the constitutional legitimacy of the EU. In a radical shift of emphasis it is possible to understand legitimacy as being *delivered* without recourse to a constitutionally defined (normative) public political space. Here there is a reliance upon providing a means of converting the concerns and questions we might have about legitimacy into definable or recognisable outputs, or ends to be achieved, and the means by which this is done. In this way legitimacy becomes a technique for delivering goals, goods or ends that can be thought about in terms of solutions or responses to the problem of achieving the specified goals of the EU.[38] Important to 'technocratic' and 'procedural' legitimacy are two elements: firstly, the expertise or expert rationality which is able to deliver efficient, optimal, solutions to meet the needs of those requiring goods, services or welfare; and secondly, that objective standards of procedural efficiency can be observed (applied), such as, transparency, consultation of relevant stakeholders, legal certainty and proportionality. What happens to constitutionalism when legitimacy is conceived in such a way becomes a vital matter to consider. However, as a basis for such a discussion of these themes, which I will return to explore throughout the book (particularly in Chapter 3), what interests us is the extent to which such an emphasis on legitimacy 'as delivery' severs the connection between constitutionalism and legitimacy as situated in a common public space.

---

36 For example, Zenon Bankowski and Emilios Christodoulidis, 'The European Union as an Essentially Contested Project', in *The European Union and its Order: The Legal Theory of European Integration*, edited by Zenon Bankowski and Andrew Scott (Oxford: Blackwell, 1999).

37 This is a point picked up and acknowledged by the pluralists themselves, see Matej Avbelj and Jan Komárek, 'Four Visions of Constitutional Pluralism', 4 *European Constitutional Law Review* (2008), pp. 524–527.

38 See Christopher Lord and Paul Magnette, 'E Pluribus Unum? Creative Disagreement about Legitimacy in the EU', 42 *JCMS*, pp. 183–202.

By suggesting that 'legitimacy as delivery' poses a challenge to constitutionalism, I do not wish to be misunderstood; it is not part of my claim that such issues of 'delivery' are not important to a political community, rather, what I am seeking to explore is whether conceiving legitimacy, in this narrow way, undermines our ability to link legitimacy with a common public space; that is to say, the fundamental link between legitimacy and a constitutional life. Part of the difficulty for constitutionalism is to think about the connection between legitimacy and political form in circumstances in which the state, as convenient shorthand for referring to a common or public space, is not unproblematically available for the EU. In beginning to locate the problem, or challenge, to constitutionalism in these terms we become mindful that what is not being sought here is a mode of settling the concerns of constitutionalism by reference to a further all-encompassing public philosophy. For while it is easy to understand how technocratic modes of legitimation sever the link with a common sense of 'public' it becomes all too tempting to re-establish such a connection by appealing to an all-encompassing, and potentially artificial, scheme of constitutionalism. Such an endeavour would, in all likelihood, present only further significant problems for the way that we understand the EU. Therefore, as a matter of urgency, it becomes important to attempt to rethink the very way in which constitutionalism is implicated in a common public space, as only by doing so can constitutionalism return to consider matters of legitimacy.

Implicating the AFSJ

How is the more specific matter of the EU's development of a common internal security policy implicated in these abstract claims about EU constitutional legitimacy? The fundamental purpose of this book is to show how the EU's area of freedom, security and justice' is a field of integration that brings to light, in a particularly vivid way, the difficulties surrounding the issue of constitutional legitimacy in the EU. By reflecting on the way that the legitimacy issues are developed in the AFSJ we will be able to learn more about the distinctive problems facing constitutionalism in the EU. We could justify this approach by simply suggesting that the subject matter of the AFSJ, internal security, is the traditional preserve of the state – after all, the development of means of controlling population and territory have been integral to the growth of state power in modernity.[39] It would appear to be this historically close relationship between internal security and the nation state which prompts Douglas-Scott to remark about the AFSJ: '[that] in the rush to further the creation of European criminal law, democratic controls

39 Michel Foucault's work has been particularly influential in establishing a historical method for understanding this shift in the distinctive form of power which he called 'bio-power'. As the state emerges the activity of governing becomes 'governmentalized' into institutions. This is a matter that I pursue in greater detail in Chapter 4.

once (sometimes) provided by the nation state have been left behind'.[40] This quote reveals how the apparent anchors of constitutional legitimacy, concerning internal security matters, become readily associated with a certain conceptualisation of the purposes of the state. However, as our previous inquiry into the wider issue of constitutional legitimacy in the EU revealed, the relationship between the concerns of constitutional legitimacy and the state is a complicated one and is not necessarily well served by relying on narrowly defined conceptual categories when examining a complicated and interrelated social totality. Indeed it becomes crucial to understand, from the developments that have taken place, the deeper sense that the absence of the state plays in the dynamics of the AFSJ, and crucially how this links to an awareness of the concern over constitutional legitimacy. With this in mind let us proceed by posing two questions, which will make clear that the concerns over constitutional legitimacy in the absence of the state are at the forefront of the tensions which drive the AFSJ; firstly, whose interests does the AFSJ represent and how? Secondly, does the AFSJ constitute a unified practice of law and politics? These two questions, as I shall set out, bring out the tensions in the development of the integration of the AFSJ as a form of concern over the constitutional legitimacy of those practices of integration in the absence of the putative political authority of the state, and also the implication stemming from this, namely that the AFSJ is intended to augment the understanding that the EU constitutes a political community beyond the state.

Who is Representing Whom?

As I previously documented, the organisation which began cooperation on internal security matters in Europe, Trevi, was a purely inter-governmental organisation; as a consequence, if one were to ask whose interests does Trevi represent, then the only possible answer could be the cooperating states. However, what is interesting about looking back to the Trevi period is that, even at this early stage, it was difficult to ring-fence cooperation on matters of internal security from political questions, and that these questions tended to come from the EC institutions. Concern was beginning to be voiced by the European Parliament that the activities of Trevi were an important area of cooperation that appeared to be outside direct democratic scrutiny. The only possible level of control was the accountability of the Justice and Home Affairs Ministers through their respective national parliaments. In a number of instances the EP attempted to draw attention to the lack of scrutiny concerning counter-terrorism measures, which were being developed by 'informal meetings'.[41]

---

40 Sionaidh Douglas-Scott, 'The Rule of Law in the European Union – Putting the Security into the Area of Freedom, Security and Justice', 29 *European Law Review* (2004), pp. 219–242 at p. 240.

41 See, for example, Resolution of the Parliament, 18 April, [1985] OJ C 122/109 and Resolution of the Parliament, 26 May [1989] OJ C 158/394.

The language of political accountability can be seen, in the light of subsequent events, to make an additional claim about whether a legitimate political interest, in the affairs of internal security, could be common to the political space of Europe. Although the possibility of this can be discerned with Trevi it becomes fully radical some years later at the Amsterdam Treaty of 1997. To that extent, it is possible to see the Maastricht Treaty (1992) as a transitional phase in which the claim to a common European interest in internal security matters was recognised, with the creation of the third pillar on Justice and Home Affairs, although the actual institutional form of the third pillar by and large preserved the pure inter-governmental character of Trevi. The development from Trevi to Maastricht also illustrates something very crucial that requires some thought: sharing technical knowledge and expertise between states on important matters of internal security raises the question of legitimacy which must be thought about in its own terms – the difficulty, of course, is to establish what thinking about legitimacy actually means and involves.

The political issues concerning internal security cooperation in Europe reached a certain maturity with the Amsterdam Treaty. In essence, the reforms made at Amsterdam allowed the EU to effectively promote and develop policy and legislation regarding internal security. Perhaps, the most tangible demonstration of this was the use of the framework decision as the legislative tool for the third pillar. Nevertheless, the third pillar continued to be largely inter-governmental in character with unanimity in Council; consultation with the European Parliament and a limited judicial review role of the Court of Justice. It was also at Amsterdam that visas, borders, immigration and asylum were acknowledged as bearing on the community freedom of movement and consequently moved to the first pillar. Having split internal security into two separate legislative regimes the policy field was unified into the 'area of freedom, security and justice'.[42] Whilst this may be viewed, by some, as a rhetorical step I consider it to have much deeper implications, since even if it was intended to be rhetorical general assumptions about political practice made the gesture meaningful and necessary. However, for the time being it is sufficient to observe that the claim to represent an area of common values is about making an assertion concerning the public interest of cooperation, which is intended to go beyond the technical questions of expertise sharing and operational goals.[43] This in turn raises a much deeper set of problems for our inquiry: in what way do we understand the meaning of 'public' in such a

42 Article 29, Title IV, TEU(M).

43 The importance of the symbolic representation of a public space in the establishment of political community is remarked upon by legal theorists in the context of the AFSJ. See in particular: Patrick Twomey, 'Constructing a Secure Space: The Area of Freedom, Security and Justice' in *Legal Issues of the Amsterdam Treaty*, edited by David O'Keeffe and Patrick Twomey (Oxford: Hart Publishing, 1999), pp. 358–359, and Hans Lindahl, 'Finding a Place for freedom, security and justice: the European Union's claim to territorial unity', 29 *European Law Review* (2004), pp. 461–484.

context? It must be acknowledged that this question goes further than accepting that the AFSJ narrative conforms to the straightforward view that what we are witnessing is an advance of the 'supranational' to the activities once carried out in the inter-governmental third pillar. The activities of the AFSJ call into question the very sense of what we mean by a 'public' interest in internal security which is represented by European institutions and law-making procedures.

The implications of the Amsterdam reforms can be seen in the immediate aftermath of the Treaty coming into force. In 1999 the European Council met in Tampere to agree measures that would serve as a blueprint for the development of the AFSJ up to the end of 2004. This was the first stage of short- and long-term policy planning for the AFSJ and consensus on the importance of internal security measures was reinforced by the perceived alterations of the security threats following 9/11 in America. The 'Hague Programme' was intended to build upon the work of Tampere but also indicates an important shift in understandings. Firstly, it was the Commission which was responsible for developing the 'Action Plan' of measures which were designed to build 'freedom, security and justice' until 2010.[44] Secondly, it is noteworthy that while many of the measures could be enacted, or developed, by the existing legislative arrangements, many of the ambitious elements of the Hague Programme anticipated the move to a supranational or Community legislative form across the AFSJ. Indeed, at the time of the Hague Programme, it was envisaged that the Constitutional Treaty would allow for the opportunity to re-cast the institutional structure of the third pillar into the 'Community' model.[45] The Hague Programme, coupled with the Constitutional reforms, indicate unambiguously that freedom, security and justice could be taken to represent the interests of the EU as a whole, and not just those of states. In this way AFSJ becomes inexorably part of the 'polity building' elements of the EU – the break with the Trevi era seems to be complete. The most recent developments seem only to provide further confirmation of this picture. The Treaty of Lisbon, born out of the failure of the Constitutional Treaty, constitutes significant structural reform for the EU.

Attempting to summarise these developments we could point to the period from Trevi to Lisbon as one in which the supranational interest has gradually prevailed in thinking about internal security. Whilst internal security began life as technical and specialist information sharing between states over time it has

---

44 See Communication from the Commission to the European Council and Parliament of 10 May 2005, 'The Hague Programme: Ten priorities for the next five years – the partnership for European renewal in the field of Freedom, Security and Justice', COM (2005) 184. Also see the joint statement by the Council and the Commission on the Action Plan for the implementation of the Hague Programme, OJL 198 (12 August 2005), pp. 1–22.

45 For a good introduction and general summary of the events and measures surrounding the development of the Constitutional Treaty see Andrew Duff, *The Struggle for Europe's Constitution* (London: Federal Trust, 2005), and see the Final Report of Working Group X, Freedom, Security and Justice, 2 December 2002, CONV 426/02.

become a policy area which defines common political goals across the EU. To link this back to the earlier points I raised, such transition becomes bound up with the uncertainties over the very possibility, and meaning, of evoking a public interest in matters of internal security. The term 'supranationalism', favoured by lawyers and political analysts alike, as a shorthand, does not approach the difficulties that are encountered. To this extent, in the task of studying the AFSJ, constitutionalism cannot be ignored and, in particular, the legitimacy of that which is taking place seems to be nothing less dramatic than the emergence of an additional political site, beyond the state, for freedom, security and justice as the commitments of a political community.

Integration and Fragmentation

If we pause for thought, however, it is clear that the development of the AFSJ is not simply a matter of ever deepening integration and an unproblematic acceptance of the EU as a political site, claiming responsibility for internal security policy. Indeed the transition from inter-governmental cooperation in Trevi to the AFSJ, to the Lisbon Treaty is equally a narrative of fragmentation. Time and again it is possible to point to instances of institutional restlessness whereby one step forward is accompanied by an equally strident step in the opposite direction. For instance, at Amsterdam the unification of the subject matter of internal security policy into the area of freedom, security and justice also betrayed fragmentation, with certain policy areas being transferred to one kind of legislative method under the first pillar, and the remaining being subject to third pillar framework. Even the extensive reforms to the AFSJ enacted by the Lisbon Treaty cannot disguise the fact that fragmentation is present in the shape of the extensive opt-outs secured for the UK, Ireland and Denmark.[46] In addition to fragmentation, illustrated in the form of 'differentiated integration' or 'variable geometry', it is also possible to find, in the new Lisbon Treaty, examples of procedures which attempt to place limits on the degree to which national interest can be overridden in respect of criminal justice matters (the old third pillar). To this extent the Commission does not enjoy a monopoly over initiative[47] but, perhaps most crucially, Member States enjoy an 'emergency' break over proposed legislation.[48] In effect this enables a Member State to place a veto over the proposed legislation in circumstances in which this would affect 'fundamental aspects of its criminal justice system'.

46 Protocol on the position of the United Kingdom and Ireland, Articles 1–4, and Protocol on the Position of Denmark. The position of the UK is particularly striking as measures adopted prior to the Lisbon Treaty have an expiry time which allows the UK to choose to opt in or out of them. For further discussion see, Maria Fletcher, 'Schengen, the European Court of Justice and Flexibility under the Lisbon Treaty: Balancing the UK's "Ins" and "Outs"', 5 *European Constitutional Law Review* (2009), pp. 71–98.

47 Article 76 TFEU.

48 Article 82(3) TFEU.

What does this 'fragmentation' point to? What might it indicate? Certainly the instances of fragmentation are not enough to suggest a wholesale apathy concerning the notion of integration regarding internal security matters. One plausible response is that fragmentation is simply an indication of the intricate negotiation over the institutional organisation and legislative powers of the AFSJ – the inevitable *realpolitik* of integration between Member States and the EU. After all, a clear-cut distinction between purely inter-governmental and supranational methods became increasingly difficult after Amsterdam.[49] For example, the institutional changes introduced to the third pillar along with the removal of asylum, visa and migration matters to the first pillar meant that the AFSJ policy area had a complex institutional and legislative matrix that incorporated features of *both* legislative methods. Hence institutional change can be said to be a highly convoluted balancing of these interests. Whilst this is plausible, I consider the issue of fragmentation goes very much deeper than disagreements over the precise form of institutional design; my argument is that fragmentation displays *concern* about the constitutional legitimacy of a policy of criminal justice, control of borders, immigration and asylum which no longer employs the sovereign state alone as the authoritative reference point for its development and meaning.

An illustration of the requirement to look behind the flux of institutional reforms and designs to get to the deeper constitutional legitimacy issues of the AFSJ can be illustrated by the case of *Council v Commission*.[50] This is a judgment that was given in a period after the failure of the Constitutional Treaty but before the signing of the Lisbon Treaty. What is of particular interest about this period of time is that during a moment of political stagnation it fell to the ECJ to provide some impetus to further the Union's aims and objectives. In a number of cases the ECJ seemed to push a 'supranational' reading of the third pillar. The issue in this particular case concerned the adoption by the Council of the framework decision 2003/80/JHA of 27 January 2003 concerning the protection of the environment through criminal law.[51] The contested framework decision stated that the Member States should take the necessary measures to criminalise certain acts that cause serious environmental damage. The ECJ stated that the framework decision was invalid since it could have been adopted as a directive on the basis of Articles 174 and 176 EC which provide that *inter alia*:

---

49 Neil Walker, 'In Search of the Area of Freedom, Security and Justice: A Constitutional Odyssey' (Oxford: Oxford University Press, 2004). For the discussion concerning the type of indices or indicants about whether a legislative process is supranational or inter-governmental, see pp. 16–17.

50 Case C-176/03 *Commission v Council* [2005] ECR I-7879.

51 Following this decision (and also case C-440/05) the recent directive 2008/99/EC ensures a wide range of environmental conduct is to receive criminal sanctions if breached. This measure is to be implemented by Member States by 26 December 2010.

> The council ... shall decide what action is to be taken by the Community in order to achieve the objectives of preserving, protecting and improving the quality of the environment.

A number of very important and controversial questions arose from this judgment. The first is that the ECJ acknowledged that the EC Treaty does bestow a competence to designate certain acts as criminal. The view had been that the whilst the Member States are often required to 'take all necessary measures' to ensure the effective and proper implementation of legislation, this fell short of actually compelling the Member States to enact criminal legislation on a particular matter. This orthodox view originated from both the absence in the EC Treaty of a reference to criminal sanctions and also the past jurisprudence of the ECJ which failed to explicitly require Member States to introduce criminal legislation.[52]

So the judgment entails significant institutional change concerning the criminal competence of the EU. Given the potentially far-reaching impact of its judgement what reasons were offered by the Court in support of its findings? The judgement is characteristically short, and the nub of the issue for the ECJ is expressed in para. 48, which states:

> [the finding that the Community does not have a criminal competence] does not prevent the Community legislature, when the application of effective, proportionate and dissuasive criminal penalties by the competent national authorities is an essential measure for combating serious environmental offences, from taking measures which relate to the criminal law of Member States which it considers necessary in order to ensure that the rules which it lays down on environmental protection are fully effective.[53]

Here we see the ECJ employs the frequently used argument of the full effectiveness of European law in order to justify the conclusions it reaches about the appropriate legal base for this measure. However, it is apparent that the controversy of the judgment is much broader than the legalistic question over which law-making procedure to use, or indeed, the level of effectiveness of European law. The deeper concern points to the extent to which we can construe, as constitutionally legitimate, the interpretation that criminal law competence can be bestowed on the Community pillar due to an argument about the effectiveness of the enforcement of European law. Does the highly coercive nature of the criminal law sanction not require a more explicit justification? And furthermore, what kind of justification would be sufficient? This last question goes deeper into the difficulties we have in conceiving how to justify criminal law which is enacted beyond the state; to recall the words of Douglas-Scott as stated earlier, 'in the rush to further the creation

52 See in particular, case 5076 *Amsterdam Bulb BV v Produktschap voor Siergewassen* [1977] ECR 137 and Case 68/88 *Commission v Greece* [1989] ECR 2979.

53 Case C-176/03 *Commission v Council* [2005] ECR I–7879, at para. 48.

of European criminal law, democratic controls once (sometimes) provided by the nation state have been left behind'.[54] Whether or not we agree with the normative implications of this statement it is apparent that our concerns centre on the challenge to conceive constitutional legitimacy in a way other than one based around the concept of the state, and that the continued development of internal security integration only serves to make this question more urgent.

Conclusion

This chapter has attempted to introduce the notion of why it is that the AFSJ is closely bound up with concerns over the constitutional legitimacy of the EU. The AFSJ claims to represent the meaning of goods, security, freedom and justice which have traditionally been the exclusive domain of the state. However, the wider question this provokes is whether, and in what ways, it is meaningful to refer to constitutional legitimacy in such circumstances? It is this attempt to work back from what is happening in the AFSJ to the way we think about the presuppositions of constitutionalism that forms the crux of the inquiry and which carries broader implications both for EU scholarship and constitutional theory. To this extent it now becomes important to clarify what meanings might be implied by using the term 'constitutional legitimacy' – to address this matter becomes central to understanding the AFSJ in constitutional terms. Having explored how we might conceive of constitutional legitimacy it will then become important to relate this back to the practices of the AFSJ to see how, or in what ways, this enhances our understanding of the constitutional issues.

To sum up the progression of the argument in this chapter, which serves as an introduction to the book, the AFSJ provokes us to think about how it is that we can establish a meaningful connection between an understanding of constitutionalism and a common public way of life when we cannot straightforwardly assume that the normative, historical and epistemological project of the state can provide an answer to this.

54 Sionaidh Douglas-Scott, 'The Rule of Law in the European Union – Putting the Security into the Area of Freedom, Security and Justice', 29 *European Law Review* (2004), pp. 219–242.

Chapter 2

Constitutional Life and Legitimacy

Introduction

Internal security integration does raise constitutional questions and, as discussed in the previous chapter, at the forefront of these the crucial matter of the legitimacy of that integration looms large. Constitutional understandings would seem to rest upon resolving the issue of legitimacy since it resides at the pinnacle of our concerns about constitutional life. Indeed it becomes plausible to claim that constitutional theory, if it has a point or purpose, *must* provide a response; it must explain how the acceptance of political power is possible. It is inconceivable that illegitimate exercise of political power through the law should be tolerated; if such a thing should happen then we must have ways of being able to alter such a situation. In the conventions of the tradition of constitutional thought this takes the form of thinking about how political power is constituted legitimately and also the constraint of illegitimate political power. It may be said, therefore, that the function of constituting and constraining power becomes a fundamental presupposition about the scholarship of constitutions. However, in the course of this chapter I intend to subject this view of constitutionalism to greater consideration. In particular, my concern is that constitutional thinking about legitimacy has tended to be focused on the scope and function of the 'constraints' on power and my claim is that constitutional theory, to the extent that it has been preoccupied by the issue of constraint, has neglected, or possibly excluded, the ontological dimensions of the question concerning the 'legitimacy' of constitutional life. I intend the ontological to carry more meaning than the general sense in which constitutionalism is concerned with collective existence. In the course of this chapter I intend to build an understanding of the ontological dimension of constitutional legitimacy as practical and situational involvements with the commitments, over time, of a political community. The attempt to think about constitutional legitimacy, in such a way that brings to the fore the ontological, leads to some unexpected findings about constitutionalism which might not otherwise have been disclosed to us.

It was above all the contested nature of the EU polity that prompted the issue of legitimacy to come to the forefront of our inquiry. In the early part of this millennium the apparent constitutional momentum of the EU towards a documentary constitution prompted some to ask difficult questions about the EU's underlying legitimacy. Neil Walker placed the question of 'polity legitimacy' as central to an understanding of the apparent momentum towards a documentary constitution.[1] Seeking a general definition of 'legitimacy' in constitutional thought, Neil Walker writes:

> By polity legitimation is meant the fundamental acceptance of the entity in question as a legitimate political community – as one possessing the authority to subject matters that significantly affect the life chances of the putative community's members to collective decision making. At the same time, such legitimation must inspire, in a related fashion (since the authority of legal and political power is inseparable from its social acceptance), a sufficient sense of social identity, or "we feeling" as to induce compliance with and thus render effective the decisions made on its behalf and in its name.[2]

Here, therefore, the meaning of legitimacy is taken to imply two elements: the *authority* to subject matters to collective decision making and the accompanying sense of *social identity* which will induce compliance. On this interpretation legitimacy is concerned with establishing an order which has the power to compel us to decide on matters together, and, as a necessary consequence, leaves us marked with a common identity. Emerging from this passage is a sense that legitimacy may be understood in both symbolic and empirical terms; as playing a role in the symbolic foundation of constitutional authority as generating a 'we feeling' of identification as evidenced by the empirical reality of compliance. Nevertheless my concern is quite the opposite and involves how authority and social identity are integral to the way we come to think about legitimacy rather than simply being the necessary symbolic components in the production and replication of compliance with the constitutional order. In this way I want to reverse Neil Walker's definition of polity legitimacy by suggesting that what 'authority' and 'social identification' actually mean is uncertain and leads us to undertake thinking about polity or constitutional legitimacy as a common involvement or engagement with the practices of constitutional life. The structure of such an engagement, as I outline in greater detail below, is hermeneutical and enables a different manner of thinking about constitutionalism. This does not rely on a conceptual representation of these terms; whereby constitutional legitimacy is assumed to be delivered as a 'product' of the reasoned legal 'constraints' or by the symbolic representation of 'we feeling' which induces compliance.

Authority, Compliance and Constraint

The transition of authority from the theological right to rule of Popes, Kings and Princes into the modern ascending theory of popular representation and consent is

1 Neil Walker, 'Europe's Constitutional momentum and the search for polity legitimacy', 3 *I.CON* (2005), pp. 201–238.

2 Ibid., p. 212.

part of the standard narrative of modern constitutional theory.[3] Nevertheless post-medieval political writers have vested their secular Sovereigns with often considerable powers of compliance and acceptance, a process which seems particularly animated by the need to keep humanity from the slavish passions of a brutish state of nature whilst satisfying those desires which have been legally recognised as constituting the subject of the Sovereign. The secular rationalism of early modernity translates the 'original sin' doctrine[4] into a conflict between 'Reason' and 'Passion' with the authority of the sovereign ensuring that rationality would prevail. Political freedom consequently is a freedom from those elements that would impair Reason and which would otherwise lead to the disruption of the civic order. 'Modern' liberty is interwoven with the constraint of passion as well as the 'irrational', and the triumph of a reasoned (and increasingly economic or 'work' based) justification for the political order.[5] Constitutional theory appears in its modern guise as the search for secular rules for the rational constraint (and organisation) of power where the ultimate source for legitimate authority ascends from the 'People'.

In one of the most extraordinary acts of the eighteenth century, the British King's subjects in the colonies of America declared independence and set about the task of establishing a constitutional settlement for their Revolution. The Constitutional document worthy of the aspirations of its age, began 'We the people', and established a means by which power could be designed so as to ensure that it does not become distorted and tyrannical. Constitutionalism became synonymous with a system of 'checks and balances' between the bases of power, ensuring that no one person or institution controlled power absolutely. For an age which was coming to know the importance of industrial machines the language of constitutionalism, as building better government by a 'system' of controls and counter-controls suggests itself very well.[6] Equally, advances in the way natural science was uncovering the laws of nature paved the way for political thinkers to consider that Reason could uncover universal laws by which man ought to govern himself and, in so doing, could free himself from accident, whim, coercion or passion and set himself upon the path of enlightened government.

The idealism of early constitutionalism may have dissipated with the realities of subsequent political experiences but the questions concerning the constraint,

3 Walter Ullmann, *A History of Political Thought in the Middle Ages* (Harmondsworth: Penguin Books, 1965).

4 For example, in the writings of St Augustine of Hippo the notion of the 'city of men', or our earthly governance, is always unjust because it is tainted by original sin.

5 Benjamin Constant, 'The liberty of the ancients compared with that of the moderns', in *Cambridge Texts in the History of Political Thought: Constant Political Writings*, edited by Biancamaria Fontana (Cambridge: Cambridge University Press, 1988). For Hegel this victory or triumph becomes dialectical and historical as the progress of the modern age is realised in the state as constitutional monarchy.

6 Martin Landau, *Political Theory and Political Science: Studies in the Methodology of Political Inquiry* (New Jersey: Humanities Press, 1979).

and organisation, of political power have retained their dominance within the development of constitutional theory. Indeed, if we were to attempt to formulate some uncontroversial presuppositions upon which constitutional understanding is based then constraint would feature very highly. For instance, we could say, without difficulty, that constitutional law:

a. vests authority in office holders and legally proscribes the basis of their power;
b. provides procedures for ensuring the responsibility and accountability of public officials;
c. separates and constrains the exercise of power amongst the political institutions; and
d. constrains legal guarantees enforcing the rights of citizens.[7]

In each of these propositions the idea of constraints and the constitution of power features prominently in any understanding of the connection between law and political liberty.

Jon Elster's work contains a powerful defence of the idea that political freedom is established due to the *foundational*, *rational* and *decisional* effort to constrain the exercise of power. In his book *Ulysses Unbound* Elster argues that it is possible that a decision taken at one point in time sets up a causal process which binds us to that decision at a later time.[8] Illustrating this point Elster alludes to the myth of Odysseus and the Sirens from the Homeric poem *Odysseus*. Sailing back to Ithaca, from the defeated city of Troy, Odysseus and his crew must safely pass the Islands of Sirenum Scopuli, home of the Sirens who lure mariners to their death on the rocks by their irresistible singing. To avoid this fate Odysseus commands his rowers to fill their ears with wax and to chain him to the mast, so that he will not succumb to the singing and steer the vessel on to the rocks. Odysseus' scheme[9] is successful and he manages to safely resist the Sirens and pass by the perilous islands. It is not surprising that this myth has become popular in constitutional theory – by constraining his authority to act, having his own men bind him to the mast under strict instructions not to release him until they are past the island, he guarantees the liberty and safety of the vessel. Elster's additional point, for

7 Taken from Sheldon Wolin, *Politics and Vision: Continuity and Innovation in Western Political Thought* (Boston: Little Brown, 1960), at p. 388.

8 Jon Elster, *Ulysses Unbound: Studies in Rationality, Pre-commitments and Constraints* (Cambridge: Cambridge University Press, 2000) at p. 43. The quote in full reads: 'a decision *t*1 counts as a way of binding oneself vis-à-vis some decision at *t*2 only if [t]he effect of carrying out the decision at *t*1 [is] to set up some causal process in the external world'.

9 I simplify the tale a bit here, as in the Homeric version Circe's divine instructions were whispered to Odysseus. The influence of the Gods in the affairs of mortals is a component of Ancient Greek belief and literature.

constitutional theory, would be that each time such a danger is encountered then this will trigger the same constraint to come into operation, ensuring that the integrity of constitutional authority can be defended against potentially damaging action.

Where does the source, or origin, of the constraint lie? Is it from the Sovereign or is it independent and prior to it? For instance, in the Odysseus example, does the authority for the constraint to bind Odysseus reside with his decision *as* Odysseus, or does it come from somewhere else, such as the common purpose to reach Ithaca? The question points to a difficulty. When we refer to constitutional constraints, are we simply referring to actual political power, and the limitation to be placed upon it, or must we implicitly consider the authority to decide on which constraints must be adopted and followed? What such concerns point to is the source, or grounding, for the understanding that the authority to decide on constraints can be distinguishable from the *power* to decide on such matters.

The contemporary uncertainty over such questions has provoked instability in the conventional understanding of constitutionalism as the institutionalised constraint on the exercise of power. In 1922 the political theorist Carl Schmitt declared that 'Sovereign is he who decides on the exception'.[10] In this phrase the logic of ultimate political freedom is ensured by the reversal of the constraint on power. In Schmitt's view the Sovereign ensures freedom, and thereby confirms his supreme authority, by possessing the power to decide outside the legal rules, procedures and constraints of the constitution. Schmitt asserts that:

> The sovereign produces and guarantees the situation in its totality. He has the monopoly over this last decision. Therein resides the essence of the state's sovereignty, which must be juristically defined correctly, not as the monopoly to coerce or to rule, but as the monopoly to decide. The exception reveals most clearly the essence of the state's authority. The decision parts here from the legal norm, and (to formulate it paradoxically) authority proves that to produce law it need not be based on law.[11]

The exceptional decision becomes a means of determining the foundational source of authority and that furthermore this foundational moment is something that takes place outside of the institutional structure of law, or the legal norm. The Sovereign, therefore, displays exceptional powers because it places the political in a primary, or 'originary', position to its foundational authority, which must then become something different from power. In constitutional theory this is identified as the site of the paradoxical relationship between the constituent power, for example of the people (*pouvoir constituant*), and the constituted power of the

---

10 C. Schmitt, *Political Theology: Four Chapters on the Concept of Sovereignty*, trans. by George Schwab (Cambridge MA: MIT Press, 1985), at p. 5. First published in 1922, second edition, 1934.

11 Ibid., p. 13.

instituted constitutional order (*pouvoir constitué*).[12] Therefore, it can be said that the authority of the Sovereign, under Schmitt's understanding, is a primordial act of decision which discloses the constituent power of the people, and, as such, is outside the constituted form of the legal constitution.

It is a peculiarity that Schmitt's articulation of power and authority resonates with another important writer of the twentieth century, whose political views and commitments were quite different. Hannah Arendt also considers that in the moment of 'beginning' an action determines the legitimacy of power – as it ascribes authority to the subsequent exercise of power through the constituted institutions of constitutional life.[13] To locate the similarity we might say that both Schmitt and Arendt sought to draw a distinction between power and authority – where the legitimacy of the act of the Sovereign stems not from any legally constituted power but from authority. Additionally, both thinkers construe authority in temporal terms – as the originary moment of beginning or foundation – which all subsequent authentic political actions can be assumed to be close to. It would seem that to understand constitutional legitimacy we must further explore 'power' and 'authority', and pay particular attention to the 'temporal' dimension of authority, contained in the works of both Arendt and Schmitt.

In part the similarities that can be found in both Schmitt and Arendt stem from the use both writers made of the Roman political experience and the scholarship of Roman Law. In Roman politics there was a clear distinction between power (*potestas*), on the one hand, and authority (*auctoritas*) on the other; this difference is apparent if we consider the phrase attributed to the orator Cicero, *cum potestas in populo auctoritas in senatu sit* (power lies with the people, authority with the Senate). The word *auctoritas* stood for the qualities that could be attributed to an *auctor*. For the Romans the *auctor* was the originator of something, rather like the way that we use the word 'author' today. Hence *auctoritas* involves developing, carrying on, or increasing[14] that which the *auctor* began. For the Roman political experience the word *auctoritas* was used as a term to convey the closeness of a political activity to the foundation or originating moment of the community – the formation of the Roman people (*Populus Romanus*) by the first King, Romulus.[15] Under the early republican constitution it was the Senate that possessed *auctoritas* and was expected to provide advice and deliberate on matters of policy; the Romans

12 For a recent edited collection of essays which contributes to the exploration of these terms in constitutional thinking, see Neil Walker and Martin Loughlin (eds), *The Paradox of Constitutionalism: Constituent Power and Constitutional Form* (Oxford: Oxford University Press, 2007).

13 Hannah Arendt, *On Revolution* (London: Penguin Books, 1990); also, *Between Past and Future: Eight Exercises in Political Thought* (New York: Penguin Classics, 1978).

14 The latin verb, *augere*, from which the noun *auctoritas* derives, means to augment.

15 This moment of foundation came with the unification of the tribes of the seven hills of the city of Rome under the first King Romulus, who was reputed to be the son of the God of War, Mars, and a Vestal Virgin.

considered this reflection concerning public affairs to be essential to the activity of politics. To understand exactly why the Senate was assumed to hold *auctoritas* it is necessary to consider its composition. Roman political society was marked by a distinction between two groups of *cives* – the Patricians or Nobles, and the Plebeians. The Patrician, or Noble families, which made up the Senate, kept their distinction from the Plebeian class by strict rules of marriage. It was a 'negotiated' settlement between Plebeians and Patricians for which the early institutional development of Rome can be seen as the balance between the interests of the old Patricians and Plebeians.[16] Aside from the material and political distinctions between Patricians and Plebeians there was also a historical distinction: according to the legend, it was Romulus, the founding King of Rome, who designated a senatorial class from the hundred or so heads of the noble families.[17] In other words, a certain social class was presumed to have a stronger link to the foundation of Rome and, therefore, to possess the *auctoritas* from the original *auctor.*

However, in order to rule it was necessary to be endowed with *potestas*; this was considered to be the specific and definable powers of a particular office, so whereas *auctoritas* could grow, or develop, *potestas* was finite and therefore limited.[18] If one were to add together all the powers and duties of the officers of state then one would obtain the total *potestas* available to government; *auctoritas*, in contrast, cannot be quantified in such a manner. Exercising the *potestas* of a particular office was to be done within the specifiable limits of the definable powers of that office, a notion that is familiar nowadays from the doctrine of *ultra vires* in public law.

The relationship of *auctoritas* to the mysterious foundation of the constituted order makes it an elusive and highly problematic political idea. In writing about the Schmittian conception of the act of the Sovereign, in deciding upon the exception, Giorgio Agamben states; '*auctoritas* seems to act as a *force that suspends* potestas *where it took place and reactivates it where it was no longer in force.* It is a power that suspends or reactivates law, but is not formally in force as law'.[19] Imputing to *auctoritas* an unlimited 'power' of action over the legally constituted order (*potestas*) brings with it considerable difficulties. Even if we are to think of *auctoritas* as something that stands outside the constituted juridical order, it is quite a different step to endow it with qualities of action, decision and power. To conflate *auctoritas* with a determinate action brings into focus the question: who wields such a power? It is very difficult, at this point, not to recall Schmitt's own

16 The agreement between the Plebeians and the Patricians became known as the *lex sacrata*, see Michael Oakeshott, *Lectures in the History of Political Thought*, edited by Terry Nardin and Luke O'Sullivan (Exeter: Imprint Academic, 2006), at p. 188.

17 Ibid.

18 Even when Augustus assumed all the *potestas* of the *Populus Romanus* this was considered to be different from *auctoritas* (which he also possessed).

19 Giorgio Agamben, *State of Exception*, translated by Kevin Attell (Chicago: University of Chicago Press, 2005). The author's emphasis.

commitment to the personal cult of the *Führer* during the Nazi dictatorship of Germany.[20] Equally, looking back further to the Roman experience, the Roman Republic eventually gave way to *Imperium* which witnessed the combination of *potestas* and *auctoritas* in the person of the Emperor Augustus.[21]

At the heart of the 'paradox of constitutionalism' we find the principal difficulty for our attempt to construe ways of understanding constitutional legitimacy. There seems to be a tendency to see the paradox of constitutionalism as manifest in direct terms: the violence involved at the foundational moment when a Sovereign is acknowledged and the legal order constituted, or alternatively, when the authentic Sovereign preserves freedom by the violent act of suspending or destroying the legally constituted order. In this way authority (*auctoritas*) becomes something that is both mysterious and immediately active; it lies beyond, or outside, the legally constituted order but can nevertheless be brought to *act* on it as a force or power that suspends or alters it. Conceiving the paradox in this way leads to a greater risk of confusion as authority becomes vulnerable to be thought of as if it were a mysterious version of power, a *symbolic* mode of enducing compliance. The confusion over authority and power can be most clearly witnessed in the infamous phrase of Schmitt, '*he* who decides on the exception', whereby *auctoritas* and *potestas* have become indistinguishable as the forces, united in symbolic power and wielded by the 'Leviathan' figure. Similar confusions between *auctoritas* and *potestas* can also be witnessed in respect of the very sense in which we evoke the *foundation* of a political community. Trying to get close to the meaning of the foundation, or beginning, of the political community can often be confused for the event, will or act of violence which brings forth something new (the activity of politics). The tendency to frame the foundation in terms of a violent decision which brings forth politics also has the capacity to obliterate any sense that we have of the foundation as something that is non-specific, and non-decisional or non-willed.

The task of thinking about constitutional legitimacy becomes a difficult one; on one level it is important to ensure that we acknowledge or recognise the importance of *auctoritas* to the constitutional life of a political people, but at the same time we must not succumb to the notion that *auctoritas* 'acts as a force' over it.

To begin to think about how to explore this issue I would like to return to the American constitutional experience. We have already stressed that American constitutionalism articulates our concerns that constitutionalism must be an

---

20 Schmitt's relationship with the Nazi Party during the 1930s and 1940s has become well documented; he beaome an influential jurist of the Third Reich and interestingly his work 'Political Theology', to which I made reference earlier, was re-published in the 1930s. For a full assessment of Schmitt's work in the context of the rise of Fascism in Germany, see John P. McCormick, *Carl Schmitt's Critique of Liberalism: Against Politics as Technology* (Cambridge: Cambridge University Press, 1997).

21 Michael Oakeshott, *Lectures in the History of Political Thought*, edited by Terry Nardin and Luke O'Sullivan (Exeter: Imprint Academic, 2006), pp. 232–233.

expression of popular sovereignty and also a framework which provides for the constraint of power – through formal constitutional mechanisms such as a separation of powers, the doctrine of checks and balances and a documentary 'Bill of Rights'. However, the American constitutional experience is also curious because, rather like that of the ancient Romans, it stresses the foundational moment of the Constitution and looks to the 'founding fathers' as authors of the Constitution.[22] It is this feature that I would like to look at now, to consider how it has become important to constitutional theory and the implications it has for our concerns about constitutional legitimacy and authority.

Although the founding moment is important to American constitutionalism it would seem that this heritage is not something that is unambiguously celebrated; in fact, there exists unease about the past having such a hold over the present. Perhaps this is because of the fact that it would seem to contradict, or at least present a contradictory message (which we explored above), to the strong constraint features of the American Constitution. Michael J. Perry expresses this concern as the 'dead hand of the past' in the following way:

> The people of the United States who did ordain and establish the Constitution in 1787–9 and the Bill of Rights in 1789–91 – are long dead. So, too, are the people who amended the Constitution in the aftermath of the Civil War. Why, then, should *we*, the people of the United States *now living*, accept constitutional directives issued by persons long dead as our 'Supreme law of the Land'?[23]

One view might be that in so far as the rules created by the founders remain 'generally accepted', as an empirical social fact, consequently we need not inquire further into their status as legitimate authority.[24] Here we return to the concern over whether authority understood simply as compliance is sufficient to convey its meaning. The difficulty is that questions over the legitimacy of the founding moment may not be so easily dismissed by supposing that, as a matter of empirical fact, modern day Americans accept and comply with the Constitution of the Founders. The issue is not so much an empirical test of compliance but the attempt to understand the relationship a particular people have to their foundational past, hence it is precisely the meaning of 'acceptance' and 'compliance' which is contentious and worthy of further thought. Frank I. Michelman suggests that it is impossible not to question the legitimacy of the role that the founding moment plays in present day constitutional

22 On the relationship between the American founding moment and the ideal of the Roman Republic, see David Richards, *Foundations of American Constitutionalism* (Oxford: Oxford University Press, 1989).

23 Michael J. Perry, 'What Is "the Constitution"?' in *Constitutionalism: Philosophical Foundations*, edited by Larry Alexander (Cambridge: Cambridge University Press 1998) at p. 101.

24 For a discussion of the legal non-volitionist view, see Frank I. Michelman, 'Constitutional Authorship' in ibid., at p. 71.

life since 'we produce an author because we have to'[25] in order to provide a grounding or basis for our constitutional life. The point being that the founding authors of the constitution must be, in Michelman's words, 'figures of rightness before they can be figures of history'.[26] This encourages us to think about the foundational moment, and also the actions of the 'authors' of the constitution, not as isolated historical events, or even figures, *but as establishing commitments of rightness over time*. At the outset it is important to realise that commitments, in this sense, are different to making a decision, choice, complying or consenting to something.[27] The authors of the foundational moment make a call about rightness, as a way of doing things in the present, which can be heard and responded to, or just as easily, may not be heeded at all. Taking the constitutional past as establishing commitments over time demands that this is a common endeavour, and recalls the views of Neil Walker, at the beginning of this chapter, that the 'we feeling' or common identity are bound up with an understanding of 'legitimacy'.

The American constitutional experience reveals that the understanding of *auctoritas* cannot be exhausted by the view which takes it to be a force (perhaps exercised by individual will) which can suspend the constituted order. *Auctoritas* is primarily a *relationship* to the foundational past whereby the core constitutional commitments are re-interpreted *over time* in such a way as to implicate a common way of constitutional life. From this understanding of *auctoritas* we can suggest that constitutional legitimacy, at the most fundamental basis, is an exploration or deliberation upon our present constitutional commitments by reference to the past, where what is at stake in this relationship is 'rightness'. In other words, legitimacy in constitutional life, to which *auctoritas* makes reference, is distinct from power or force, because it is a kind of thinking, reflection or deliberation about how rightness is enfolded into the present, by a common commitment *over time*, in the activity of politics. For instance, in the Republican era of Rome, the Senate was said to hold *auctoritas* because it was composed of elders who were presumed to *be able to reflect on the meaning of the legitimate foundation*, and what this required as guidance for the particular moment – they gave sound advice. Nevertheless, reaching this stage in our understanding of constitutional legitimacy raises a further, and perhaps more challenging problem: does the ensuing sense of constitutional authority, as a commitment to rightness, simply become a 'product' of the symbolic means for ensuring the compliance with the constitutional order? In other words, we meet the difficulty that authority is simply viewed as a means by which 'compliance' with the constitutional order can be assured by guaranteeing the symbolic dimensions of constitutional life, as commitments, inducing a 'we feeling', to borrow once again from Neil Walker's phrase. Without further addressing what *kind of deliberation* is implied by these 'commitments to

25 Ibid., p. 92.

26 Ibid., p. 81.

27 That is to say the idea of legal authority as offering 'reasons for action' from the work, principally, of Joseph Raz.

rightness' the notion of constitutional authority (*auctoritas)* once again becomes vulnerable to being construed as a symbolic power to be wielded by the 'figures of rightness'. Hence the crucial question, for the next section, is in what way can deliberation preserve the *distinctiveness* of constitutional authority as something *intrinsic* to our concerns over constitutional legitimacy?

Before moving to consider these questions it might be appropriate to summarise, briefly, the current direction of the argument. The rational legal constraints on the Sovereign, which form the basis of modern thinking about constitutionalism, leave unresolved the question of what basis the constituted order is founded upon, because the very notion of 'foundation' becomes problematical. Legitimacy, understood as the primordial and foundational experience of political freedom, occurs outside the constituted power, and therefore undergirds its authority. Hence legitimacy cannot be reduced, and so understood, according to the institutions, procedures and officials which are thought to constrain political power. Taking the Latin word *auctoritas* for the authentic foundational experience of a political community this was in turn contrasted with the definable, finite and specific powers of the constitutional order, *potestas*. I argued that there are very grave problems about conceiving *auctoritas* to be a force that suspends the constituted order, and indeed, it would appear to be highly problematical to assert that *auctoritas* could be wielded by a Sovereign will. Hence our route to understanding legitimacy, as the foundational experience of political authority, must in fact lie with understanding the relationship between authority and the idea of living with the commitments of rightness undertaken by the political community.

Hermeneutics and its Implications

Let us further explore the notion that constitutional legitimacy is a reflection, or a deliberation, upon the distinctive commitments of a political activity which implicates both time and collective existence. To this extent we are concerned with the meaning of these constitutional commitments, or at least the interpretation of them, and how such commitments become a means of ensuring that we have a sense of *being* a political community. In coming to this point I have found the tradition of hermeneutics to be central to any significant reflection on these issues. In this section I offer a summary of the development of hermeneutics as an intellectual endeavour, and, in particular, I propose to consider how the hermeneutics of Hans-Georg Gadamer becomes relevant to exploring constitutional legitimacy.

Deep within the tradition of hermeneutical thinking is the recognition of the predicament facing humanity of a fundamental alienation from meaning and the attempt to overcome this.[28] The word, hermeneutics, is related to the name of the

28 Hans-Georg Gadamer, 'The Universality of the Hermeneutical Problem', in *Philosophical Hermeneutics*, translated and edited by David Linge (Berkeley: University of California Press, 1977).

Greek God Hermes. In the Platonic dialogue *Protagoras*, we are told that Zeus, fearing men would destroy themselves due to their maladaption to the world, sent Hermes to teach all men the virtue of Justice (*Dikē*) so that they could, at least, live in a community with each other.[29] It is suggestive that hermeneutics is implicated, in this Plato dialogue; not only in respect of the meaning of civic life, but also through the ultimate alienation that takes place between man and his environment. It is understood that the means of overcoming this fundamental alienation is language or communication (*logos*) and so hermeneutics, for Aristotle, becomes a mode of dealing through language: addressing, communicating, conversing and interpreting.[30]

Interpretation became crucial in the history of hermeneutics with the need to interpret the texts of God, the *logos* of God,[31] a task which gave great weight to hermeneutics as a recovery of God's word and our alienation from Him. In this way hermeneutics is no longer simply civic communication but a technique of interpreting sacred texts. In the nineteenth century hermeneutics was further refined into a general technique, as a way of developing a rigorous epistemology for the study of historical consciousness. In the works of Schliermacher understanding presupposes a common language and that the object of understanding is a 'fact' in the thinking mind of another. Hence, recovering meaning, from a text, becomes a historical exercise into the cultural context of the work but also a psychological investigation as to the intentions of the original author. Both these features of hermeneutical science were developed by Wilhelm Dilthey who made a concerted effort to explore how knowledge of the historical consciousness is possible, a claim to universal hermeneutics.[32] Two expressions become central for Dilthey in this search for an epistemological grounding to historical consciousness: *Erlebnis*, or experience, and *Zusammenhang*, or interconnection (continuity). Above all

29 It is also worth noting that a number of fragments of a play by Aeschylus seem to further our understanding of this myth. It would seem that Zeus awarded the gift of justice to men due to a 'deal' struck with Prometheus, see Hugh Lloyd-Jones, *The Justice of Zeus* (Berkeley: University of California Press, 1971), pp. 94–103.

30 See Martin Heidegger, *Ontology: The Hermeneutics of Facticity*, trans. John van Buren (Bloomington: Indiana University Press, 1999) at p. 7.

31 St John's Gospel I. 1–5, 'In the beginning was the Word, and the Word was with God, and the Word was God. The same was in the beginning with God. All things were made by him; and without him was not anything made that was made. In him was life; and the life was the light of men. And the light shineth in darkness; and the darkness comprehended it not'.

32 It is also worth being aware that around this time there were also those who sought to find a theological vision to the notion of historical consciousness; writers like Ranke and Burkhardt refer to the historical unity of the world, and J.G. Droysen addresses the 'moral power' latent in historical development. Theological visions of history, in this way, point us towards ontological questions – or at least show how post-Hegelianism developed along a sort of theological–historical line that presupposed the universality of hermeneutics and also its relationship to emerging questions of 'being'.

exploring these concepts involved a psychological search into the experience (*Erlebnis*) of the inner life of the 'minds' of the past, of the author, or thinker, by the signs left behind in such a way as we come to know our interconnection (*Zusammenhang*) with the works of the past. It was then, in part, through an attraction towards the burgeoning developments in the field of psychology that Dilthey thought he could base a reconstruction of the 'minds/life' of the past so as to lead to the perfect interpretation of the texts left to us.[33]

Hermeneutics, as a recovery of the historical consciousness of ancient texts, lends a certain confidence to the view that the human sciences could be placed on an epistemologically sure footing and that the alienation from the historical process could be resolved. It is a claim that sees the 'hermeneutic scientist' as the subject investigating an object (a text) via a technique that will lead to an objectively valid meaning for that text. As a mode of understanding it ensured that hermeneutics remained close to conventional notions of subject–object of study and to presuppose that truth was a correspondence between words used and the factual disposition of the author's mind.

A fundamental shift in hermeneutics began when Martin Heidegger moved from concerns over methodology and epistemology to address matters of fundamental ontology. In his early lectures on hermeneutics, *hermeneutics of facticity*,[34] he sought to connect hermeneutics back once again to questions of existence through language:

> In the title given to the following investigation, hermeneutics is *not* being used in its modern meaning, and in no sense does it have the meaning of such a broadly conceived doctrine *about* interpretation. In connection with its original meaning, this term means rather: a definite unity in the actualising (of communicating), i.e., of the *interpreting of facticity* in which facticity is being encountered, seen, grasped and expressed in concepts.[35]

The implications for an ontological basis for hermeneutics, in the human sciences, were investigated by Heidegger's pupil, Hans-Georg Gadamer, principally in the book *Warheit und Methode* (Truth and Method). It is Gadamer's contribution that will form the basis of my own attempts to demonstrate the importance of hermeneutics for constitutional theory – and, in particular, our concern about a sort of deliberation which discloses our relationship to commitments over time. The wider issues concerning the relationship between Gadamer and

33 Incidentally such ideas are not confined to the German historical school but constituted a widely followed European 'idealist' movement; for instance, the views of Dilthey are very similar to those of Robin G. Collingwood in Britain, see in particular, *The Idea of History* (Oxford: Oxford University Press, 1994), and Benedetto Croce in Italy, see *Teoria e Storia della Storiografia* (Bari: Laterza, 1973).

34 Martin Heidegger, *Ontology: The Hermeneutics of Facticity.*

35 Ibid., p. 11.

Heidegger – which represents an interesting avenue of investigation in its own right – are beyond the scope of this book. It is known that Heidegger's lectures on hermeneutics, which Gadamer draws on extensively in *Truth and Method*, constitute his very 'early work' and that much later, even after the publication of his most famous tract *Being and Time*, Heidegger's work was to explore the neglected question of Being which lies beyond the existence of objects, practices, entities and the conventional metaphysical subjects of Western Philosophy. Gadamer's philosophy on the human sciences owes a considerable debt to Heidegger's work in the phenomenological study of Being; however, the existence of such a relationship does not mean that Gadamer's own contribution cannot be studied in its own light.

The abandonment of the nineteenth century concerns to provide a universal hermeneutics, grounded on an objective epistemological footing, frees hermeneutics from a number of presuppositions which enable it to be re-invigorated as a mode of understanding about the meanings of social and political practices.[36] It is important to understand the sorts of presuppositions that are rejected by hermeneutics, developed by Gadamer, in order to enable a better appreciation of the implications of this approach to understanding social and political practices.

Object-Subject Distinction

In the earliest traditions of hermeneutics the object of study was a text, typically a sacred one, and there was presumption of a fundamental distinction between the subject (or knowledge seeker) and the object of knowledge. Later, in the tradition of hermeneutics, the object of knowledge changed to the historical consciousness, but the distinction between subject and object remained. The distinction is a deep cultural tradition of thought[37] and indeed it is difficult not to understand the past as displaying shifts in material or power which become the object of our study. Nor is it without precedent to ascribe to history, or our social practices, a kind of purpose or point which orientates an understanding of it as a theoretical object of investigation. So pervasive is this distinction that it becomes difficult to envisage a form of thinking or understanding which does not, to some extent, compel us to make what we are thinking about an 'object' of our studies.

---

36 Hans-Georg Gadamer 'Scope and Function of Reflection' in *Philosophical Hermeneutics*. It is noteworthy that Gadamer refers to this as philosophical, as opposed to ontological hermeneutics – it suggests a different project to the one developed by Heidegger; nevertheless, the ontological direction taken by Heidegger is essential to enable Gadamer to make the arguments that he does concerning the importance of hermeneutics in the study of the humanities or *Geisteswissenschaften*.

37 It is often referred to as 'Cartesian'.

In the tradition of hermeneutics, understanding the text as object of study involved addressing the particularities of the text in terms of the whole, and the whole in terms of the particularities. By a process of going back and forth, in such a way, a complete mastery and understanding of the text would emerge. This technique, dubbed the 'hermeneutical circle', envisaged that each text contained a sort of self-sufficient meaning to be grasped. However, the 'hermeneutical circle' becomes problematic when we ask how are we to locate an 'objective' standpoint from which to distinguish one correct interpretation from another? Or another way of posing the same issue is to ask whether an objective criterion can be found within the text or is identified by some external methodology? If there is indeed no external criterion for adjudicating the veracity of one interpretation over another then we may well wonder whether this does not present a decisive problem for hermeneutics. Gadamer attempted to break away from the conventional understanding of hermeneutics by making the problem of the 'hermeneutical circle' a springboard for showing something fundamental about the activity of making interpretations. In an indication that Gadamer owes such an insight to the ontological shifts in hermeneutics developed by Heidegger he quotes a passage from *Being and Time*:

> It [the hermeneutical circle] is not to be reduced to the level of a vicious circle, or even of a circle which is merely tolerated. In the circle is hidden a positive possibility of the most primordial kind of knowing, and we genuinely grasp this possibility only when we have understood that our first, last, and constant task in interpreting is never to allow our fore-having, fore-sight and fore-conception to be presented to us by fancies and popular conceptions, but rather to make the scientific theme secure by working out these fore-structures in terms of the things themselves.[38]

It is apparent that the interpretation must be directed towards the 'things themselves', that which involves our interpretation, and in doing so we are to be vigilant against arbitrary 'fancy' or conventional opinion. However, what is most noteworthy about this quote is that when a person is interpreting a text he is *projecting* onto it his 'fore-having, fore-sight and fore-conception'.[39] In other words he is *making* an interpretation from his own fore-knowledge (his background understanding), and it is the inevitability of this that Heidegger counsels caution over in the above quotation. In Gadamer's work the projection of fore-knowledge in interpretation becomes centrally important since it is the fore-knowledge of our understanding

38 Quoted from Gadamer, *Truth and Method* trans. by Joel Weinsheimer (London: Continuum Press, 2004) at p. 269.

39 'fore-having' meaning something we have in advance; 'fore-sight' meaning something we see in advance and 'fore-conception' meaning something we grasp in advance. Martin Heidegger, *Being and Time*, trans. by John Macquarrie and Edward Robinson (Oxford, Blackwells, 1962), p. 191.

that constitutes the very basis of our understanding as immersed in 'tradition'.[40] Another way of expressing this might be to say that any understanding always takes place from a *point* of knowing, or a situation of understanding. This will be developed later when we come to discussing the related idea of the 'fusion of horizons'. Gadamer seeks to emphasise that contrary to Enlightenment views concerning rationality the event of understanding is one in which we bring our fore-knowledge to a situation rather than seeking an objective technique of mediating between ourselves and the thing we are interpreting. Gadamer sees in this event 'a process of transmission in which past and present are constantly mediated',[41] which is a moment when a *relationship* between interpreter and that which is being interpreted is constituted:

> The circle, then, is not formal in nature. It is neither subjective nor objective, but describes understanding as the interplay of the movement of tradition and the movement of the interpreter. The anticipation of meaning that governs our understanding of a text is not an act of subjectivity, but proceeds from the commonality that binds us to the tradition. But this commonality is constantly being formed in our relation to tradition. Tradition is not simply a permanent precondition; rather, we produce it ourselves inasmuch as we understand, participate in the evolution of tradition, and hence further determine it ourselves. Thus the circle of understanding is not a 'methodological' circle, but describes an element of the ontological structure of understanding.[42]

Interpretation is construed as a *relationship* in which the interpreter and the 'thing itself' becomes implicated in an activity of understanding in which both become less strange or alien to each other. This comes about by an open and questioning stance, but also by the acknowledgement of the inevitability of the background or tradition being projected onto our activity of interpretation. The science of hermeneutics means acknowledging that the past, present and also future possibilities occur as a common event of understanding which is not methodological or abstract in nature, but instead is *practically transformative* of what we have usually termed the 'subject' and 'object' of interpretation. Hence, the use of the word tradition, which can so often become misunderstood, is not the attempt to confine the past to mean a static object. Rather it is to make the past move with the shifting horizons of our own understanding and so bring it to the foreground of our thinking and acting, and so involve us in a relationship with it – which is both transformative of the tradition and those who seek to understand it. It is a relationship of understanding which emphasises learning rather than the desire to either grasp the 'object' or submit to being the 'subject' of the object.

40 Hans-Georg Gadamer, *Truth and Method*, p. 278.

41 Ibid., p. 291.

42 Ibid., p. 293–294.

Truth as Disclosure in Application

It may be assumed that because hermeneutics does not put forward a method or technique, by which objectively correct interpretations can be known, it can have no conception of 'truth'. A problem, it might be thought, lurking within hermeneutics is that if each view or opinion is equally valid then as such there can be no assessment as to whether one interpretation is necessarily more meaningful than another, the consequence being more a cacophony than something resembling intellectual thought. The difficulty is, in fact, somewhat deeper than such an easy criticism would suppose because an idea of hermeneutics which understands the 'object' of study as being in a transformative relationship with the 'subject' seeking knowledge of it must also develop quite a different notion of truth to the one that we may conventionally acknowledge. When we use the word truth, conventionally, we tend to employ a formulation which corresponds or coheres with an 'object' which we are attempting to understand – this object, as we have discussed, may be a text, or it might be a complex social or cultural practice – and so truth, in the conventional sense, relies upon both the validity of the statement as corresponding to the object and upon maintaining the distinction between them.

The difficulty becomes apparent: it is common to rely upon an idea of truth which must preserve the distinction between a 'subject' and an 'object' if there is to be something like a standard of truth. If hermeneutics is to get beyond this issue, for the human sciences, then this must be a way of understanding a notion of truth in circumstances, as in the activity of interpreting, when truth becomes disclosed as a relationship or an 'event' of understanding between the interpreter and a text or social practice. Gadamer comes to express this as a 'fusion of horizons' of understanding. This way of knowing also acquires an importance, for Gadamer, since we recall that the hermeneutic event, from which the truth emerges, is fundamentally understood as an encounter with the horizon of tradition:

> Every finite present has its limitations. We define the concept of situation by saying that it represents a standpoint that limits the possibility of vision. Hence essential to the concept of situation is the concept of horizon. The horizon is the range of vision that includes everything that can be seen from a particular vantage point ... A person who has no horizon does not see far enough and hence over values what is nearest to him. On the other hand, to have a horizon means not to be limited to what is nearby but being able to see beyond it. A person who has a horizon knows the relative significance of everything within this horizon, whether it is near or far, great or small. Similarly, working out the hermeneutical situation means acquiring the right horizon of inquiry for the questions evoked by the encounter with tradition ... thus the horizon of the past out of which all human life lives and which exists in the form of tradition,

> is always in motion. The surrounding horizon is not set in motion by historical consciousness. But in this motion becomes aware of itself.[43]

I have quoted this passage at length in order to indicate how truth, in the hermeneutic event, is a disclosure of the horizon of possibilities by the projection of fore-knowledge (our situated understanding) in a dynamic relationship. The quote above vividly conveys the notion that the truth of the interpretation is a *moving* engagement and the word 'fusion' itself captures this notion of motion. A little further on in this passage Gadamer continues to outline the notion of the horizon of understanding:

> In the process of understanding, a real fusing of horizons occurs – which means that as the historical horizon is projected it is simultaneously superseded. To bring about this fusion ... is the task of what we called historically effected consciousness ... it is in fact the central problem of hermeneutics. It is the problem of *application*, which is to be found in all understanding.[44]

It is significant that Gadamer draws attention to this moment of truth as being 'an application' and therefore truth seems to be part of an on-going activity of 'application'. A difficulty for Gadamer is to fully account for the meaning of the term 'application' as the basis of a hermeneutic understanding capable of disclosing the truth of the 'interpretive event'. Gadamer does so by drawing a distinction between two words that feature prominently in Aristotle's *Ethics*,[45] *technē* (τεχνη) and *phronēsis* (φρονησις), but which acquire an interesting new place in Gadamer's understanding of hermeneutics. According to Gadamer, for Aristotle, *technē* is the exemplary form of knowledge which is used by a craftsman who knows how to make a specific thing. The craftsman has a plan (*eidos*) of the thing which he is going to make, or construct, and the materials which he is going to use to that end,[46] whilst *phronēsis* becomes a practical knowing, or wisdom, which is always responsive to a particular situation. Gadamer interprets this distinction between these forms of understanding as relevant to the hermeneutic application. Whilst *technē* is a genuine and authentic form of knowledge which requires skill and experience it does not resolve the problem of the hermeneutic application. Recalling that interpretation is a relationship whereby the interpreter projects an interpretation and is also affected by that which he is interpreting shows us that we cannot make ourselves to be at the disposal of a plan which we project onto to ourselves – for it is in fact imperative that we remain open to the particular encounter in the hermeneutic event. Hermeneutics is a practical knowledge, or

43 Gadamer, *Truth and Method*, pp. 302–303.

44 Ibid., p. 306.

45 Aristotle, *Nicomachean Ethics of Aristotle*, trans. by Sir David Ross (London: Oxford University Press, 1954), in particular, see Book VI.

46 Gadamer, *Truth and Method*, p. 313.

wisdom, which is responsive not to a plan but to the sensitivity to the particular moment (the point that the horizons do become fused) and what demands this makes of us to respond. It is apparent that Gadamer's main preoccupation is not to clarify how these terms were used in ancient Greece but rather to indicate something about our own mode of understanding and to draw our attention to the limits of what we might call 'theoretical' or 'technical knowledge'. It is possible to see the contrast between 'technical' and 'practical' knowledge in the following distinctions used by Gadamer:

- Theoretical knowledge is acquired and learnt but may also be forgotten. However, practical knowledge is not something we can choose to acquire since we are already in the situation of acting or deciding – it is the situation that presents to us the unique way in which we must respond knowingly.
- Crucially, theoretical knowledge is always directed towards particular ends whereas practical knowledge cannot serve specified ends but must be directed towards to those ends that are disclosed as right in the situation. The means by which this is achieved cannot be taught, or knowable in advance of confronting the situation.
- Practical knowledge has a unique relation to itself, such that it is rather like a conscientious advice giving which is insightful or sensitive to the situation. Gadamer writes that 'we say that someone is insightful when they make a fair, correct judgment. An insightful person is prepared to consider the particular situation of the other person, and hence he is also most inclined to be forbearing or to forgive. Here again it is clear that this is not technical knowledge'.[47]

Hermeneutics emphasises a notion of truth which is situated in our past, or in traditions, which are disclosed by interpretations in the present. These interpretations re-cast tradition in such a way that we can say that the past is not static but always moving according to the use we make of it in our present interpretation. Our understanding is a relationship between the inevitably of the background which we project onto our interpretation and the realisation that we are encountering future possibilities. It is a relationship which, if it is to be disclosed and understood, requires thinking which is not technical, or calculative, but instead is a practical knowledge in the sense that it is not directed towards meeting specific or planned ends, or goals, but is always open to the unique situation, the encounter with the phenomenon being interpreted and the demands such a moment makes upon us.

As a way of returning to the specific concerns of this chapter in respect of constitutional legitimacy, it is worth noting that Gadamer emphasises that the hermeneutic experience is one that always entails an encounter with another – 'A

47 Hans-Georg Gadamer, *Truth and Method*, p. 320.

Thou'.[48] Gadamer refers to the hermeneutical experience as being a 'conversation' or a 'partnership' with another – not as an object to be understood or pitied, but as a conscious 'Thou' in dialogue. The recurrences of the terms 'conversation' or 'dialogue', in Gadamer's work, are not accidental but rather indicate that the basis of any hermeneutical experience is language. The non-private medium of language in which all questions and answers must be expressed is the site upon which hermeneutic relations take place, 'our inquiry has been guided by the basic idea that language is a medium where I and the world meet or, rather, manifest their original belonging together'.

Conclusion: Constitutional Life

Recalling the decisive question that directed our search towards hermeneutics, how are we to understand the distinctive deliberation of constitutional commitments over time that implicates our sense of political belonging? Crucially the answer to this question must approached in ways that are different from the organisation of 'power' through the constituted legal order or from the symbolic authority intended to induce compliance with the constituted order. In the course of taking this different approach to constitutional thinking I rejected two possibilities. Firstly, authority could not be understood as an institutionalised structure of constraints because this inevitably compels us to accept arbitrary or unquestionable 'foundations' for such an order. It was apparent that such a paradox over the legitimacy of the constituted order was exploited by Schmitt in his remark about the Sovereign being the one who decides to suspend the constituted order. However, this second understanding had not only the difficulty of equating authority with an object – the will – but equally it appeared to suggest that authority was a 'force' or 'action' which addresses itself towards determinate ends or goals, such as the suspension of the constituted order. In my argument the preferred way of understanding authority is as a distinctive form of deliberation – which I took to be the common commitments of the political community *over time*. Hermeneutics reveals, I contend, how we can construe this 'distinctive deliberation', upon which the authority and legitimacy of constitutional life can be sustained. The insights that hermeneutics, and in particular the work of Gadamer, brought to light can be summarised in relation to four themes by which we can think about constitutional legitimacy.

- The 'foundation' (which tends to be construed as the decisional act of power) and the constitutional commitments that occur over time are a crucial component of constitutional practice. However, such commitments must be approached not as historical objects for theoretical understanding but as traditions under which the political community exists in a relationship of interpretation. Such commitments, although developing out of the past,

48 Ibid., 352.

are not static but rather move or change according to our interpretation of the shared past and the unique, or particular, requirements of the present situation. Commitments are living possibilities and not fossilised records of the past moments of a constitutional life.

- Constitutional commitments are a medium by which we relate to others, not as separate 'subjects' or 'consumers' but as partners in an on-going conversation about the meaning and application of the commitments to a common constitutional life. Such a relationship 'discloses' the meanings of constitutional life through practical understanding.
- Constitutional commitments are guides to action and therefore cannot be understood to stipulate a specified end or outcome. In this way constitutional commitments are 'disclosed' on the basis of practical knowledge as the response to a particular situation. A truthful interpretation, therefore, aims to 'disclose' how our constitutional commitments guide towards possible responses to our situation. This is in contrast to applying a technique (*technē*) to direct the constitutional practice of commitments towards specified ends, goals or principles (this encompasses descriptive and normative theoretical projects). By thinking about commitments as forming a practical vernacular of constitutional life they can be understood as being *inherently valuable* since they are part of how we experience our constitutional world and not because they can be used as a means of achieving a goal, project or end – no matter how apparently appealing we may find such a prospect. Lastly, the insights of hermeneutics indicate that being together, as a political community, as a practical and situational relationship, is transformative of how we understand constitutional authority and our involvement with it.
- Lastly, the insights of hermeneutics emphasises that there can be no distinction between the 'object' of understanding and the 'subject' and, therefore, constitutional authority cannot be understood as an 'object'; likewise our involvement with it cannot be construed as the 'subject' determined by the constituted order. The route to thinking about constitutional legitimacy is to understand the extent to which we become participants in shaping the meaning of our collective lives and in so doing transform our own understanding of ourselves.

The common commitments which are inherently valuable, and participation in disclosing their meaning, which changes over time, is the basis of constitutional life. In this way the hermeneutic understanding of the question of constitutional legitimacy strikes a different note to those which are conventionally adopted in constitutional theory. However, the task is to explore a different vocabulary and thinking about constitutional legitimacy in order to be able to better understand the practices and difficulties of the relationship between the AFSJ and constitutionalism. Hence, the recourse to hermeneutics, in this chapter, has only been valid in so far as it offers different ways of thinking through the difficulty of constitutionalism in the context of the so-called 'post-state constellation'. The next chapter seeks to explore ways in which the AFSJ, as an important component of EU integration, does represent or articulate the constitutional commitments of the EU as a political community – once this has been established we can begin to engage with the practices of such commitments. Therefore, it becomes crucial, in the chapters that follow, not to lose connection with the ideas about constitutionalism explored during the course of this chapter – as they will become central to how we can think about the constitutional legitimacy of the practices taking place in the EU's area of freedom, security and justice.

Chapter 3
Public Goods as Constitutional Goods

Introduction

This chapter begins from the position that the public goods of freedom, security and justice, in the AFSJ, come to be understood as a constitutional commitment of the EU. It has already been revealed how the AFSJ has become implicated in the questions concerning the constitutional legitimacy of the EU (Chapter 1) and in the previous chapter (Chapter 2) we set out how we can begin to think about what is essential in the question of constitutional legitimacy. In this chapter the transition is made to consider more directly the constitutional issues of the AFSJ; which will orientate the approach towards the substantive matters of this book. This chapter explores the understanding of public goods with a view to indicating how a common area of security, justice and freedom becomes central to understanding the practices of the AFSJ in constitutional terms, and more specifically, as commitments to constitutional goods.[1]

To begin with it is important to resolve some reservations we might have about the relationship between the kind of thinking about constitutionalism that I explored in the previous chapter, and what we know about the emerging, or embryonic, sense of constitutionalism of the AFSJ. The most apparent difficulty in making the connection is the issue of time. Thinking about constitutional legitimacy entails involvement in commitments over time; this was termed the 'traditions' of the political community. I claimed that it was tradition which formed a background of constitutional experience, and was considered to be the basis of how we can think about the *authority* of, and *identification* with, the political community. However, this emphasis on temporality seems to sit very awkwardly with a practice of constitutionalism, in the AFSJ and EU, which is comparatively recent and where both the authority of and identification with the political community are consequently weak or even disputed (an issue which we were particularly occupied with in Chapter 1). The EU (and its antecedent the EC) is just over 50 years old and the AFSJ, as an auxiliary part of this constitutional practice, was established with the Amsterdam Treaty of 1997. To compound the problem EU constitutional practice, as we have already acknowledged, exists alongside the much more historical and developed tradition of the state. Not only does this make

1 For a discussion of freedom, security and justice as the goods of a political community, see an earlier article that I wrote related to the idea of conceiving a 'balance' between security and freedom/justice considerations: Alun Gibbs, 'Reasoned Balance in Europe's Area of Freedom, Security and Justice', 17 *European Law Journal*, pp. 121–137.

it difficult to think about the autonomous constitutional commitments of the EU but also the very language of 'tradition', 'time' and 'foundation' seem conspicuously out of place in the post-national context of EU constitutionalism. The risk being that, in the circumstances surrounding the political practices of integration in the EU, linking constitutional legitimacy with the 'past' or 'tradition' leads towards the risk of a pastiche of genuine constitutional commitment, or, at best, a sort of eccentric irrelevance (such as the various attempts at the symbolism of common commitments: the 'Ode to Joy' anthem and the 'Unity in Diversity' motto for example).

It is clear, then, that constitutional commitments, which emerge through our involvement in tradition, must be capable of greater depth if they are to be the basis of thinking through the serious concerns about the legitimacy of that which is taking place within the EU – and the focus of our study, the AFSJ. To take this path I would like to make explicit two matters which arose in the previous chapter, but which may only now acquire significance in terms of our concerns. Firstly, when I refer to the notion of 'tradition' what I do not intend to indicate is something necessarily historical. For example, I do not consider a constitutional commitment as being qualified, or identified, as such simply because it can be found to take place over a historically long period of time. Similarly the nature of the specific commitments of a political community cannot be understood simply because they are historical – i.e. by attempting to grasp its historical meaning or the historical context from which it emerges. This is not the same as saying a historical analysis of constitutionalism cannot be adopted at all; it is simply that this will reveal little about the nature of the *practical* involvement with the commitment that is the focus of our inquiry here. In this way it is crucial to realise that the constitutional commitments, founded by the AFSJ, do not disqualify themselves simply because the AFSJ is *historically recent*; as temporality, in this sense, is not our direct concern here.

Secondly, constitutional commitments are not to be confused with the notion of 'constitutional values' which implies a normative or evaluative theory of constitutional legitimacy. For instance, in constitutional studies of the European Union it is frequently asserted that the programme of integration can be said to be founded to realise such values as 'peace', 'prosperity', 'respect for the rule of law' or 'constitutional tolerance' which are taken to be the normative basis for how we might evaluate the constitutional practice of the EU. Normative theories, such as this, may serve to give a teleological coherence to European integration but may also serve as a basis for a broader evaluative grounding for the legitimacy of the EU itself (an example of such an approach is Joseph Weiler's understanding of the EU as exemplifying value of 'constitutional tolerance'). As I attempted to indicate in the previous chapter, what we are seeking with constitutional commitments is a mode of revealing the meaning of the commitments by our *practical involvement* in interpreting the practices of these commitments. This I view as being different from seeking a normative theory of the practice of EU constitutionalism, as a whole, which purportedly evaluates and directs this practice. An important task of this chapter, consequently, becomes the clarification as to what 'practical involvement' might mean as a way of constituting the meaning of public goods.

Having offered these clarifications about the ambit of the terms 'constitutional commitments' and 'tradition', I would like to indicate a bit more clearly the focus of this chapter. My claim is that freedom, security and justice are goods which can be thought about as common constitutional commitments over time, and I refer to this as constitutional public goods. As a consequence the primary purpose of this chapter entails showing how the goods of security, freedom and justice can be understood as common commitments of the EU. In doing so I intend to highlight a crucial distinction between this, constitutional, way of understanding public goods, and a different way, which I shall term 'instrumental goods'. Whilst it is part of my claim that it becomes important to make a sufficient distinction between the different ways of understanding public goods, it is not part of my argument that the constitutional mode of understanding public goods is necessarily better than 'instrumental' public goods. Indeed, a proper understanding of goods, as instrumental, might be valid and also an inescapable part of modern political communities whereby we rely on the political to deliver needs and interests. However, it must not be assumed that this is the path to constitutional legitimacy, or, that dwelling on the problems of the instrumental delivery of public goods will necessarily displace the urgency of thinking about goods in constitutional terms. In fact, the crucial matter to realise, from the point of view of constitutionalism, is that the distinction between instrumental and constitutional approaches to public goods must be established if we are to properly engage with the question of the meaning of constitutional legitimacy at all. It is this precise question which has become vital in the context of the AFSJ, and the question which we must keep in sharp focus.

What do we mean by Instrumental Goods?

To begin to consider the kinds of understandings I refer to when I use the term 'instrumental public goods, let us take as an example the sort of everyday scenes or circumstances in which I might encounter a number of public and private goods. Suppose I am walking out of my office to buy a new book. On my way I pass by a municipal park and the police station, where I notice that a police officer is helping a foreign visitor. I buy my book and on the way back I stop in my local coffee shop to buy an espresso before going to the Public Library to read my book, consult other books and talk to some friends who like to work there. In this typical scene I have encountered a range of private and public goods. I have purchased my book and coffee – these are goods that are supplied to me alone by contractual arrangement. However, I also benefitted from public goods, which I may contribute to, by way of paying taxes, but which are not restricted in their supply. For instance everyone, including the foreign visitor, benefits from the police force providing law and order and likewise every resident (whether paying tax or not) can enjoy access to the municipal park or the cultural repository of the public library. It is also worth pointing out that my enjoyment of the municipal park, or the public library, is not necessarily at anyone else's expense – if I visit Hyde Park on a Thursday morning I am not limiting, restricting or depriving other Londoners from the enjoyment of visiting the park on that very day (assuming of course that the entire population of London does not decide to visit all at once).

This is a simplified account of the sort of understanding of public goods that emerges in economic literature. Mancur Olsen writes that what characterises public goods is 'non-excludability' also 'non-rivalness'. Law and order is a common example, once the Government provides a system of policing and the military then this is available to all and does not exclude people from the benefits of law and order even though they may not be paying taxes – contributing directly to the public good. For economics it is apparent that the idea of non-excludability is a means of understanding matters relating to the efficient or optimal consumption and production of public goods and, in particular, the difficulty of how we can design a system to 'dis-incentivise' the 'free-riding' approach taken by those who enjoy the good but do not bear the burdens (perhaps mainly financial) of provision and delivery. Whilst these are undoubtedly very pressing questions for economists, and additionally policy makers, they do not directly concern those with an interest in constitutionalism unless it is in the purely mundane sense in which any political authority may coerce its population into contributing to collective projects. What is of greater interest, however, is the understanding of the words 'public' and 'good' that emerges, and whether such thinking about the meaning of 'public' is capable of revealing dimensions about the way in which we understand notions of collective authority. It is part of my contention that this classical economic understanding of public goods is what I shall call 'instrumental' and that this must be understood as being different from a constitutional understanding of public goods. The nature of this difference between an instrumental and a constitutional understanding of public goods becomes the task of this chapter. To begin with I would like to explore the 'instrumental' understanding of public goods by outlining how this approach leads to a distinctive understanding of the meaning of 'public' and 'goods' and crucially the sort of agency the individual enjoys in such an understanding. It is my view that there are four prominent presuppositions that characterise the instrumental view of public goods: technological contingency; individual need; resource/goal orientation and techniques of delivery. Ultimately it is possible to understand that the relationship between 'public' and 'good' is one that is causal and that the basis of our agency is that of 'using' or 'consuming'.

Technologically Contingent

Let us first of all take a classical, and hopefully uncontroversial, example of a public good; namely, law and order. Perhaps it is apparent that our conception of the range of possibilities of what 'public' means in this example of 'law and order' is pretty well secure and assured. Firstly, it seems almost axiomatic that we all require law and order so that we may live securely in a political community and, secondly, it does appear to be essentially a public phenomenon – the law and order infrastructure once established benefits everyone. However, if we carefully consider the issue we realise that our sense of 'publicness' is contingent on the market or technology *not* being able to provide 'law and order' as a private good. To quote from the economist Olsen, 'it is not necessary that exclusion be technically impossible, it is only necessary that it be infeasible or uneconomic'.[2] In other words, depending on technological advancement, the capabilities of the market, or indeed other unforeseen 'impossibilities', the market may be able to offer exclusive (private) provision of what was once thought of as a 'public' good. This market provision of the public good may exist in a supportive capacity, that is to say alongside any collective provision, or alternatively may in fact completely displace the public provision. Take for example, the currently burgeoning industry of 'private' security which is not in substitution for the public good but exists alongside it.[3] Hence, it is possible to see that under the instrumental view our understanding of 'public' becomes very vulnerable (contingent) to material changes, particularly in relation to advances in technology or what the commercial market is prepared to supply exclusively to individuals.

Individual Need and Interest

A further feature of the instrumental view of public goods is that the question concerning what the good actually *is* can be settled by identifying and calculating the individual interest, or need, in respect of the good. Charles Taylor writes that the individual interest approach, in understanding public (he calls it social) goods, relies upon an 'atomistic' conception of good. What this 'atomism' entails is that the fundamental basis for making qualitative assessments about the 'good' is the extent to which this 'good' meets a purported interest or need of the individual. Consequently, it can be said that the individual becomes the convenient 'unit' of measurement in respect of the meaning of 'public'.[4] Consider the following quotation which indicates how this is typically expressed by the economics literature:

> Finally, we assume that the individual's demand curve for any given collective good is similar to his demand curve for a private good. Thus, after some point the individual receives decreasing marginal utility from the consumption of

2 Mancur Olsen, *A Theory of Groups and Organizations* (Cambridge, MA: Harvard University Press, 1965) at p. 14.

3 See references to private security and the sociological and criminology work on this issue in Ian Loader and Neil Walker, *Civilizing Security* (Cambridge: Cambridge University Press, 2007) at pp. 22–23; 64–66; 126 and 136.

4 Charles Taylor, *Philosophical Arguments* (Cambridge, MA: Harvard University Press, 1997), Chapter 7 'Irreducibly Social Goods', at p. 127.

> additional units of any given collective good. That is the more the individual has already consumed, the less he values the receipt of an additional unit of the same good.[5]

It is possible to appreciate that the advantage of taking the individual as the basic unit for determining the public good is because it enables the instrumental dimension to make accurate calculations as to resources concerning the levels of need which are required to be fulfilled. This may be combined with determinations as to the 'selection' behaviour of the 'unit' which in turns allows for sophisticated patterns, or calculations, to be made in a manner that is useful, or indeed essential, to those who must make policy decisions regarding delivery or distribution.

Resources and Ends

What are the implications of this understanding of the 'good' as the needs, or interests, of the individual? Fundamentally it becomes possible to ascertain that the 'good' is assumed to be a resource to be ready at the disposal of individuals. This may also imply that we take the 'good' to be finite or determinable. Taylor reflects on this, suggesting it entails a 'consequentialist' view of goods – in other words, we can make assessments about the public good by studying the definitive result or consequences. A simple example of this might be that the provision of public good 'y' was deemed to 'satisfy' 98 out of 100 people consulted. Of course, we may further consider how we measure, or verify, 'satisfaction', but the point is that if we understand the good as a resource which caters for individual interests then we can carry out studies as to exactly how this good does meet individual needs and interests. Therefore, the techniques and methods of delivering goods, and obtaining data about such delivery, become all important to the understanding of goods.

Techniques of Delivery

The relationship between 'public' and 'good', understood by the instrumental approach, implies specialist knowledge as to the 'delivery' of individual needs and the management of the resources of the public good in question. Such a question is relevant, and of the utmost concern, for those involved in policy decision making and also those who are developing this knowledge framework in educational institutions. Academic and professional disciplines, within modern social sciences, are particularly involved in developing and supporting the delivery of instrumental public goods by seeking to define the conceptual parameters of

---

5 Norman Frohlich, Joe Oppenheimer and Oran Young, *Political Leadership and Collective Goods* (Princeton, NJ: Princeton University Press, 1971) at p. 32. Collective goods (or social goods) are defined as public goods that could be delivered as private goods, but are usually delivered by the government for various reasons, including social policy.

delivery.[6] For example, in the example above public good 'y' was supposed to 'satisfy' 98 out of 100 customers, therefore, part of the technique of delivery is to seek a stable conceptual definition of 'satisfaction' in order to be able to compile accurate statistical data concerning the delivery of public good 'y'.

What characterises public goods, understood instrumentally, is that the relationship between 'public' and 'good' is one of cause – whereby what is 'public' is something which brings about or efficiently delivers the specified individual interest (good). 'Public' therefore has a limited meaning which, as we observed, may be contingent upon material or structural limitations in the means of delivery. To this extent we can see how the term 'instrumental' becomes relevant because 'public' becomes a means (the instrumental framework) to achieve the 'good' determined by individual interest.

Thinking about public goods instrumentally is a necessary feature of current political practice – indeed it would be hard to envisage a modern political community that does not face the challenge of delivering public goods efficiently to a citizenry that claims legitimate personal interest in such matters as a police force, public libraries, and so forth. We are well aware that to establish an area of freedom, security and justice rightly raises such questions as: 'What sort of measures are going to be introduced to ensure I am safe from organised criminality in Europe?' or 'How are you going to protect the external borders of the European Union?' There can be little doubt that to think about freedom, security and justice, in modern Europe, is to be compelled to think about them as instrumental public goods.

In addition to establishing a causal understanding of the relationship between 'public' and the meaning of 'good' the instrumental public good implies a particular way of conceiving the agency of the individual, or we might also say the engagement or involvement with the good. The first mode of engagement in the instrumental good would be one in which we were able to set the theoretical or technical parameters for the delivery of the public good. To do this we may be the formulator of public policy or provide the theoretical and technical resources of delivery. As such we might think of involvement, in this sense, as a professional facilitator of the provision and delivery of the good which meets the needs or interests of individuals. The second sense in which we may understand our agency of an instrumental public good is as the beneficiary in the supply of the good; our agency here may be located as simply the individual who obtains the benefit of the good and, therefore, is in receipt of a satisfaction. In addition the agency of the beneficiary of the good may be expressed through the record of a commentary on how well, or otherwise, the professional facilitator delivered the public good (maybe in order to improve the technical delivery of the public good on future iterations). It is noteworthy that in no circumstance can either sense of agency (as a professional facilitator or beneficiary) in an instrumental public good actually become a participant in the *meaning* of the good itself, for the reason that I gave

6 Particularly in relation to economics and sociology.

earlier that the relationship between public and good was causal rather than one of meaning.

To think of public goods instrumentally is not, however, to think of them as 'constitutional public goods'. This is the crucial distinction that I seek to make. It is tempting to assume that the issues of constitutional legitimacy can be resolved provided that we are meeting the collective need for the provision of public goods. This cannot be the case. For public goods to be capable of providing constitutional legitimacy – for public goods to be constitutional commitments – we must also think about them constitutionally. As I shall make clear, in the following section, constitutional public goods are much more foundational than instrumental public goods because they do not establish a relationship of cause between 'public' and 'good'; instead constitutional public goods conceive the relationship as one of *meaning* and support or foster an agency of practical involvement in that meaning. To this extent, however, there is a significant limitation that must be acknowledged because to give public meaning to goods, as part of addressing constitutional legitimacy, entails abandoning a sense that we can have any significant technical or methodological control over this attribution of meaning. Although constitutional public goods may be understood to be more foundational, or more basic to a political way of life, in other ways attempting to articulate how these are important as part of our thinking and acting on our constitutional life is equally as complicated and challenging as those questions concerning the technical delivery of collective needs. This is partly due to the acknowledgment, which we explored in the previous chapter, that understanding constitutional commitments is a distinctive *practical* activity but also related to this we may tend to neglect to acknowledge the significance of constitutional public goods precisely because the technical challenges of instrumental public goods tend to occupy our concerns. This latter aspect of the difference between instrumental and constitutional goods becomes clearer in the next chapter when we consider the particular problems over the status of 'security' as a public good.

Constitutional Public Goods

The first step towards exploring an understanding of constitutional public goods is to expand upon the claim that it is our practical involvement with 'goods' which reveals the constitutional commitments made by a political community. Two questions immediately arise: firstly, what is meant by *revealing* the constitutional commitment (and therefore the meaning of the good)? Secondly, what sort of *involvement* is required to reveal the constitutional commitment? It is thinking through the implications of these questions that will lead to understanding how constitutional public goods are quite different to instrumental public goods. Developing the insights of the previous chapter, about the ontological dimension of constitutional legitimacy, I intend to demonstrate that it is the involvement with the 'goods' of a political community that establishes constitutional commitments over time and that crucially this engagement occurs through language.

To think about the relationship between 'good' and 'public', as one of meaning rather than cause, begins by addressing public as inherently valuable and not just because it delivers, through its institutional structures, goods which are needed by individuals. It must be valued intrinsically as the site where we involve ourselves as constituting the 'good' as a 'good'. In such a way the 'public' is a site where meaning is constituted. The 'public' is a strange place because it is not the site of technique, nor can it be the place of the calculation of individual interest or need; rather it is where we practically involve ourselves with the commitments of the political community over time and where we bring forth the possibilities of meaning for our constitutional commitments.

Revealing Constitutional Public Goods – Language

The Canadian political philosopher, Charles Taylor, bases his understanding of public goods on how we make assessments or evaluations as to whether something is worthwhile or not. He claims that our expressions of worth become possible by drawing upon a common 'social background' which we might also, on the basis of the previous chapter, term tradition. The focus of Taylor's approach concerns the role of language in enabling us to recognise these background social meanings and thereby form views about the possibilities about certain modes of living. Taylor illustrates this argument by using the examples of 'bad' historical novels which fail to take into account 'background meaning'. For example, if we read that a man in a Neolithic village thinks that his lover is 'sophisticated' or a character from the early Middle Ages rejects a course of action because it is not fulfilling, then we might think this is not very plausible.[7] It just could not be possible for those characters at that time and in those situations to be thinking, saying or doing those things. The reason being that those meanings did not exist for them; such persons lacked the language resources and crucially the background meanings to arrive at the conclusion that a lover could be 'sophisticated' or that a job could be 'unfulfilling'.

Due to language it is also possible to appreciate that meaning events have a two-dimensional quality; they are particular events, but only in relation to a background meaning.[8] For Taylor this is the basis for the distinction that Saussure draws between *langue* and *parole*.[9] The overall code of *langue* depends upon the individual acts of speech (*parole*), and so there is a basic inter-dependency, or circularity, between the acts of *parole* and the overall language code (*langue*).

---

7 Charles Taylor, 'Irreducibly Social Goods', *Philosophical Arguments* (Cambridge, MA: Harvard University Press, 1997), at p. 131.

8 Ibid., p. 134.

9 Ibid., see also, Ferdinand de Saussure, *Cours de Linguistique Générale* (Paris: Payot, 1985) in particular, Chapter 4.

Hence acts of *parole* constantly confirm or recreate the background of *langue*, for instance, where misspeak and deviant usage catches on and becomes accepted as part of the wider language code. Despite this interdependence Taylor does not want to collapse *langue* completely into *parole* – because *langue* remains 'not an individual matter but the normative practice of a community'.[10] Taylor's principal contention is that there is an irreducible social element that simply cannot be decomposed to individual acts, results or events:

> Methodological individualistic accounts of social processes have to break down because they can't cope with this fact. In one sense, perhaps, all acts and choices are individual. They are, however, only the acts and choices they are against the background of practices and understandings. But this langue can't be reduced to a set of acts, choices or indeed other predicates of individuals. Its locus is a society. This is the undecomposable kernel against which atomism must break its teeth.[11]

It is possible, therefore, to appreciate that there is an irreducible public component to the way we make judgements about whether something is a 'public good' and the sorts of meanings attached to the notion of the 'good':

> (1) the goods of a culture that makes conceivable actions, feelings, valued ways of life, and (2) goods that essentially incorporate common understandings of their value.[12]

What becomes apparent, from this way of framing the issue, is that it is the 'background meaning', or tradition, which actually *constitutes* or establishes the value or good of something and consequently enables us to form conclusions about the *different possibilities* that are before us. In this way Taylor's use of the term background meaning is similar to the way hermeneutics understands 'tradition', that is to say not as the historical presuppositions of a culture but rather as the open-ended and potential meaning generated by a 'practical' mode of being-together as community – as opposed to the determinate order of 'delivering' individual needs and interests. A similar view of the importance of the 'public' in *constituting* the meaning of the good can be located in Joseph Raz's work, in which he argues that there must be a way of understanding 'goods' which cannot be made subject to the aggregation of individual interests; he terms such goods 'inherent':

> General beneficial features of a society are inherently public goods. It is a public good, and inherently so, that this society is a tolerant society, that it is an educated society, that it is infused with a sense of respect for human beings

10 Charles Taylor, 'Irreducibly Social Goods', at p. 134.

11 Ibid., p. 136.

12 Ibid., p. 140.

> etc … The benefits I have in mind are the more diffuse ones deriving from the general character of the society to which one belongs … and cannot be directly controlled by individuals.[13]

'Revealing' as Involvement

It is claimed that the 'good' can be constituted by the 'public' and that furthermore this is a relationship of meaning determined by tradition and not individual interest or need. It is on this basis that we can think about public goods as constitutional and not simply instrumentally. However, the full understanding of public goods, in the constitutional sense, has not yet been stated because whilst we have commented that the understanding of 'good' cannot be made by reference to the individual interest what we have not done is indicate much about the involvement we do have, as individuals, in shaping the constitutional public good. Another way of putting this would be: on this understanding what does it mean for me to possess a practical agency in forming the meaning of a public good if this meaning has nothing to do with my direct needs or interests?

Such a question is of genuine concern because once it is accepted that the constitutional public good does not have anything to do with individual needs and interests the difficult question emerges as to whether the 'individual' disappears altogether and we are simply left with notions of tradition and collective agency. And, if so, what actually are we if not a beneficiary capable of making a claim on the provision of a good on the basis of our felt need? Consider in this context the voices of concern expressed first by Charles Taylor and then by Joseph Raz:

> Now let us say that each act of parole can be attributed to an individual or (decomposably) to individuals (I am not sure I want to concede this at the end of the day, but it seems a common sense assumption).[14]

> To suggest that living in a tolerant society is a good independently of its consequences, that is intrinsically good is, in their opinion, to reject humanism, for it amounts to the intrinsic value of something which is not human life or its quality.[15]

Do these misgivings reflect a serious tension in our understanding of constitutional public goods or can we think about the kind of involvement that the public good calls on us to make? Clearly it will be a different sort of involvement to the way that we understood the instrumental public good but in what way? These questions reflect the concerns that we must legitimately resolve if proceeding with

---

13 Joseph Raz, 'Right Based Moralities' in *Theories of Rights*, edited by Jeremy Waldron (Oxford: Oxford University Press, 1984), at p. 187.

14 Charles Taylor, 'Irreducibly Social Goods', at p. 134.

15 Joseph Raz, 'Right Based Moralities', at p. 188.

thicker notions of public good is to be considered an appropriate response to the instrumental conception of public good.

If we consider the problem carefully it is clear that the idea of 'tradition' or 'background' does not constitute the meaning of the good in a straightforward sense – if it were to do so then it would be an intolerable and rigid controlling force. If 'tradition' were to be conceived as *de facto* providing us with meaning then we may worry that 'tradition' or background becomes a source of formulaic truth, rooted in strict rituals or routines intended to offer strict parameters of behaviour and thought. Tradition may indeed come to be seen as a means of providing a deep psychological need for security and continuity in such a rigid way due to the circumstances of 'flux' that we tend to find ourselves in modern societies. As the sociologist Anthony Giddens writes:

> There is no logic, or moral authenticity, to doing today what one did yesterday; yet these things are the very essence of tradition. The fact that today we can become addicted to anything – any aspect of lifestyle – indicates the comprehensiveness of the dissolution of tradition (we should add, and this is not as paradoxical as it seems, in its traditional form). The progress of addiction is a substantively significant feature of the postmodern social universe, but is also a negative index of the very process of the detraditionalizing of society.[16]

The danger is that by 'blindly' following a tradition of practice – simply repeating what we did yesterday time and again – tradition becomes a symbolic order administering formulaic truth and psychological dependency. To claim that constitutional public goods rely upon 'tradition' or 'background' for meaning in order to sustain the relationship between 'public' and 'good' does indeed risk being misunderstood. It now becomes important in our analysis of tradition to establish the kind of agency that we enjoy when our constitutional lives can be said to be constituted by tradition. If we consider the quotation from Anthony Giddens, above, it is clear that to understand that any conception of the subject as psychologically dependent upon constitutional commitments is unlikely to be a satisfactory conception of practical involvement in constitutional life. Indeed, it points to a difficulty of establishing a vocabulary to refer to 'individual involvement' where we may be quite unfamiliar with exactly the sorts of involvements that do not purport to represent us as dependent subjects upon the satisfaction of a delivered good (that is the involvement that characterises our involvement in instrumental goods). The difficult task, therefore, is to consider how we establish an understanding of the activity of 'revealing' the meaning of public good, based on tradition, which is not formulaic or rigid but does depend upon a conception of *agency*. This becomes crucial because it is easy to appreciate that the search

---

16 Ulrich Beck, Anthony Giddens and Scott Lash, *Reflexive Modernization: Politics, Tradition and Aesthetics in the Modern Social Order* (Cambridge: Polity Press, 1994), at p. 71.

for a traditional way of life (i.e. *not* the present) which can be the source of truth, direction and meaning in fact becomes a means of delivering an individual or collective need and so renders tradition an instrumental public good.

In furthering our understanding of the agency entailed by constitutional public goods Denise Réaume writes that understanding public goods involves re-configuring how we come to understand our involvement so as to move away from the conception that the 'good' fulfils a need or interest but rather our practical involvement becomes the good itself:

> The value of such a good [cultured society] is partly constituted by a particular kind of participation. Such goods, which I shall call 'participatory goods' involve activities that not only require many in order to produce the good but are valuable only because of the joint involvement of many. The publicity of production itself is what is valued – the good *is* the participation.[17]

A cultured society is not a set of artefacts – plays, paintings, films. The good does not consist in some end product, such as clean streets, which, once in existence, can only be externally related to its enjoyment as means to ends; it consists in participating in the production of those artefacts which constitute a cultured society. But there is no end product because, in a sense, these artefacts are never completed but are continuously reinterpreted and recreated by each generation. This is the essence of a cultured society and can only take place *through*, not simply *because* of, the involvement of many.[18]

Réaume argues that involvement is an activity of participation – so, for instance, if we consider the example of the good of 'culture' it is possible to clearly understand that the meaning of the good rests upon participation – making films or attending the cinema, playing a musical instrument or going to a music concert. However, the crucial aspect to grasp is that these various cultural activities are not ends in themselves and nor can such activities, in isolation, be considered to fulfil or disclose all that can be meant by a 'cultured society' but instead are 'continuously reinterpreted and recreated by each generation'. In other words, our involvement with the good is *open-ended* and indeed our task, or perhaps burden, is actually to ensure that we can pass this 'open-ended' good of culture on to successive generations; only in so doing will involvement in the good be 'for itself'. This *open-endedness* not only applies in relation to the meaning of the good which cannot become fixed or rigid due to continued active engagement but equally the modes, or manner, of our active engagement which cannot become prescribed or fixed as to how the meaning of the good will be revealed. This also recalls the crucial dimension of involvement, developed in the previous chapter,

---

17 Denise Réaume, 'Individuals, Groups, and Rights to Public Goods', 38 *The University of Toronto Law Journal* (1988), pp. 1–27, at p. 10.

18 Ibid., p. 11. Author's own emphasis.

in which an engagement, or relationship, of understanding, in the hermeneutical sense, was transformative of both the 'object' of understanding and the 'subject'.

To summarise the recent discussion: 'tradition', on the basis of which we come to understand the meaning of the public good, is open ended and demands that each generation is responsible for re-interpreting and re-creating it by practical involvement. In other words, it is only through open-ended participation that 'tradition' has any meaning to afford successive generations and the effect of converting it into an 'end', by asserting that it is a source of formulaic truth, would be to diminish its capacity to be *meaningful* for us since it would restrict our involvement in it.

At this point it remains for us to clarify what is meant by practical involvement – what is the basis of the agency of participation in the open-ended meaning of the constitutional public good? It is helpful to return to the work of Charles Taylor, in his collection of essays entitled *Human Agency and Language*.[19] Taylor develops the understanding that, in its most primordial sense, participation, the exercise of agency, will emerge through language – our practical involvement can only come through linguistic expression. Taylor draws upon certain insights made by Harry Frankfurt.[20] According to Frankfurt it is not unusual to find that other species have desires and to some extent make choices, but what is distinctively human is the ability to make assessments and evaluate those desires in order to determine a course of action.[21] However, Taylor wishes to explore this further and enquire as to the sort of assessments or evaluations humans make about their practices, as distinct from simply suggesting that evaluations are simply linked to needs and desires, an aspect that we explored earlier. Accordingly Taylor argues that there are two senses in which we can understand assessments: the first he calls 'weak evaluations' and the other he terms 'strong evaluations'. In making weak evaluations we are basically concerned with outcomes, with bringing things about, whereas strong evaluations are those that are concerned with the quality or worth of our desires.[22] Let me now explore in a little bit more detail how we might understand this distinction.

For a weak evaluation, assessments are primarily conducted on how much certain contingencies correspond with our desires. Taylor gives the example of

19 Charles Taylor, *Human Agency and Language: Philosophical Papers Volume 1* (Cambridge: Cambridge University Press, 1985). It is also interesting to see certain ideas about language and social meaning linked to the issue of the way we form a sense of human selfhood, see Charles Taylor, *Sources of the Self: The Making of the Modern Identity* (Cambridge: Cambridge University Press, 1989).

20 Harry Frankfurt, 'Freedom of the Will and the concept of a person', 67(1) *Journal of Philosophy*, pp. 5–20 quoted and discussed in Charles Taylor, 'What is Human Agency?' in *Human Agency and Language*, at p. 15.

21 Ibid., p. 16.

22 Charles Taylor, 'What is Human Agency?' in *Human Agency and Language*, at p. 15.

going on holiday somewhere; whether we go to the south for relaxation (for the beach) or to the north for exhilaration (for outdoor activities). We know that the motivation for selecting the holiday is going to be different; rest in one case and exhilaration in the other. A decision between these two will be conducted on how well the holiday will be projected to meet our desires on grounds of contingency and so on. In this sense it is not that we calculate in any utilitarian way between the different alternatives; it is just that we do not carry out assessments of worth concerning our motivations.[23] 'Weak' evaluations therefore correspond broadly to how we understood the development of our needs and interests in instrumental public goods.

A strong evaluation is one that operates at a level of 'depth', whereby we make statements as to worth and value. In order to comport ourselves towards such assessments we possess a rich vocabulary of qualitative contrast; for example, 'noble or base', 'integrating or fragmenting', 'courageous or cowardly', 'clairvoyant or blind'.[24] For Taylor, this rich contrastive language about how we determine our choices also can be said to constitute our experience – simply 'certain modes of experiencing the world are not possible without certain self-descriptions'.[25] Meaning derives from the rich array of qualitative language to share or develop things in common between ourselves, thereby experiencing our agency in the world.[26]

It is language that forms the basis of our involvement – it is the 'medium' of our practical interpretive experience.[27] If our speech enables us to participate in the meaning of public goods then this implies that we must be attentive to the range of expression available in language. In particular, it becomes of urgent concern if language no longer provides an 'open-ended' sense of possibility – if expression becomes closed, or lacking, in 'qualitative contrast', to use Taylor's phrase. If this were to transpire then our participation in the meaning of our shared political life would become comprised. Therefore, being in the midst of language requires vigilance to foster the medium we possess in order to preserve our sense of agency in the formation of public meaning. Sustaining the public space relies upon the care of language, which is able convey the intimations concerning the

23 Ibid., p. 17.

24 Ibid., p. 19.

25 Ibid., p. 37.

26 This idea of the poverty of language leading to the limitation of our sense of human agency is vividly portrayed by George Orwell in the novel *Nineteen Eighty-Four* (London: Penguin Books, 1954). In order to dominate the way people think, the Party, in Orwell's novel, invents a new language, Newspeak. In Newspeak, one word is able to serve for all purposes – the 'destruction of words'. For instance, good can express bad by becoming 'ungood' and to express really bad becomes 'doubleplusungood'. In other words the most effective control that party can employ is to invent a language that does not have a rich range of words to express qualitative contrast.

27 Hans-Georg Gadamer, 'Language as the Medium of the Hermeneutic Experience', in *Truth and Method*, pp. 385–493.

extent of our experience of living constitutionally. Rather like the way in which we understand constitutional public goods as different from instrumental public goods, so too must we be prepared to confront the extent to which our political language can also be richer than expressing need, interest and contingency. The constitutional public realm prompts us to respond to our experience of involvement with constitutional public goods through language.

The call to ensure our political practice remains 'open ended', by ensuring that the language of political experience remains rich in order to give voice to our constitutional life also implies that we think about the 'public space' as the site of such political experiences. In Hannah Arendt's work, the *Human Condition*,[28] there is a reminder that the institutional presuppositions about the technical apparatus of the modern state ought not to restrict us from recognising the open possibility of what the open public space can be:

> … the reality of the public realm relies on the simultaneous presence of innumerable perspectives and aspects in which the common world presents itself and for which no common measurement or denominator can ever be devised … Being seen and being heard by others derive their significance from the fact that everybody sees and hears from a different position. This is the meaning of public life, compared to which even the most richest and most satisfying family life can offer only the prolongation and or multiplication of one's own position with its attending aspects and perspectives'.[29]

Recognition of our participation in the meaning of constitutional public goods entails that we call into question the 'public' space. However, it does not necessarily follow that calling into question the dimensions of the public space somehow entails or results in a critical and programmatic project of reform. It is not a question of arming ourselves with a critical vocabulary or, indeed, to seek a *tabula rasa* of new possibilities. Rather what is especially called for is a waiting or a patience concerning the public space; the emphasis of the open-endedness of both the meaning of goods and the manner of our involvement with them must also mean that the 'public' itself becomes open-ended. Whilst this may seem strange, at first, it merely becomes necessary to recognise that aspects of what we consider to be 'fixed' components of public organisation may simply be episodes or stages of it. This is particularly relevant for a study of the EU whereby to acknowledge the concerns of constitutional legitimacy is to recognise the distinctive form of 'public' constituted by such practices (see earlier, Chapter 1). Therefore, involvement in constitutional public goods does not become the basis for critical thought, in the sense that we constantly seek to re-make our political life by a technical procedure, but rather for a patient release from such a gesture

28 Hannah Arendt, *The Human Condition* (Chicago, IL: University of Chicago Press, 1998).

29 Ibid., p. 58.

of control. Instead, involvement becomes recognised as a stewardship over the language capable of expressing different possibilities of practically engaging with the commitments of constitutional life. Whilst falling short of an understanding of programmatic reform this notion of constitutional public goods nevertheless holds open the possibility of different ways of constituting our political lives, and this includes the relationship with instrumental ways of conceiving public goods. Such openness to release from wholly instrumental thinking may also hold the possibility that we are able appreciate and place limits on the way we conceive our demands for the delivery of needs and interests (as we shall see, this is particularly important in understanding the AFSJ in relation to the good of 'security'). Consequently, in developing our sense of constitutional life it becomes vital to seek to preserve the integrity of the public space as an 'open place' where meaning and language can indeed be confronted as the basis upon which any common political life can be practised despite the inevitable pluralities of all human communities. It seems this points to the ultimate paradox of constitutionalism: that its most difficult task is precisely to ensure that the public space is at its core (in language), unconstituted or unfounded.

Conclusion

In this chapter I have offered two radically alternate conceptions of public goods – one instrumental and the other constitutional. Whilst I stressed that these must be thought about differently I have also claimed that the goods of freedom, security and justice can be *both* instrumental and constitutional. The AFSJ *may* deliver on its claim to be an 'area of freedom, security and justice' through offering a programme of measures which provides responses to our instrumental needs, such as, to ensure that transnational crime is properly prevented or that common evidential protections are in place for those accused of crimes. We may rightly contest and question whether what is proposed will achieve such goals but we must acknowledge that the EU, through the AFSJ, has claimed the role of internal security 'provider' alongside the state. However, this is not all there is to say on freedom, security and justice in the AFSJ. As well as such a role, public goods, as has been acknowledged in the first chapter, become implicated in wider questions about the constitutional legitimacy of the EU. Freedom, security and justice become emblematic of the way a distinctive political space and experience is constituted and it is the unfamiliar character of this that causes us concern. This way of thinking reveals that freedom, security and justice are also constitutional public goods. And this in turn raises the critical question: what is, therefore, the relationship between the instrumental understanding of freedom, security and justice as public goods and constitutional understanding?

It is by posing such a question that we encounter the issue of importance for constitutional thinking. It is my claim that the distinctive aspect of our involvement with constitutional thinking, which I have developed in this chapter, allows us to consider the 'balance' between instrumental public goods and constitutional public goods. In other words, it is through participating in constitutional public goods that we also place limits on our instrumental understanding of goods and may also alter the way in which we understand goods as being instrumental. It is the constitutional public goods which impose limits on instrumentalism because fundamentally instrumentalism does not acknowledge any internal limits on its capacity for delivery – instrumentalism constantly strives to overcome the technological and market contingencies that place arbitrary limitations on its capabilities.

It is only through constitutional life that it becomes possible to think about the limitations of instrumentalism in order to provide its tendency to dominance in its mastery of determined needs and interests. In fact to put the matter more concretely the 'good' of constitutionalism demands that we impose limitations on instrumentalism by a different way of thinking and practising that explores the dimensions of constitutional life.. However, it is equally important that limitations on instrumentalism emerge from practical involvements or judgements and not from a programmatic instrument of change.

That any political community must conceive public goods *both* instrumentally and constitutionally provides a new perspective on our reflections concerning the way we make judgements concerning constitutional legitimacy. In the previous chapter, following closely the work of Hans-Georg Gadamer, a sharp distinction was drawn between understandings which were theoretical (*technē*) and those which were based upon practical wisdom (*phronēsis*). Whilst our work in this chapter augments and supports the basis of practical wisdom, or as we have termed it practical involvement, as central to the understanding of constitutional public goods, however, our reflections on public goods, including instrumental public goods, reveal that a political community can be faced with complex inter-relationships between technical reason and practical engagement. A sharp distinction between technical knowledge and practical involvement has the potential to mislead in so far as we assume that our understanding of technical knowledge is immune from alteration by practical engagement[30] and conversely that practical engagement can be corroded such that it becomes simply a prior know-how concerning compliance with the political order.

It now becomes possible to narrow our constitutional concerns over legitimacy. To what extent are we able to think about freedom, security and justice as constitutional public goods? How are we able to think about the relationship between instrumental and constitutional understandings of such goods? I hope it is possible to appreciate that these questions are a more specific way of posing the issue that we started out with, in Chapter 1, in respect of constitutional legitimacy of the EU and the extent to which the AFSJ was implicated in this.

30 This brings to the fore the Heideggerian position about *technē* not as control or mastery but as revealing, see 'Building, Dwelling, Thinking' in *Basic Writings*, edited by David Farrell Krell (London: Routledge, 2010).

To begin to consider these issues it is important, firstly, to ask whether there is a significant problem about conceiving security as a constitutional public good. There is already a significant body of academic literature which is sceptical of the role of security; particularly as to whether it is, in fact, inimical to the public good. It becomes critical to look at this issue first before trying to assess, more generally, how we are approaching the practical involvement with constitutional public goods in the AFSJ.

Chapter 4
The Public Good of Security

Introduction

In the last chapter the relationship between constitutional legitimacy and a balancing or judgement between an instrumental and a constitutional understanding of public goods was put forward. This chapter marks something of a shift in emphasis whereby we begin to explore, and engage with, the practices of the AFSJ in greater detail based upon the approach already outlined in the previous chapters. This chapter therefore becomes a bridge between our reflections about constitutional legitimacy and the scrutiny of the practices of the AFSJ. It is the problematical status of the public good of 'security' that will be explored here in this chapter. In particular, it becomes important to ask why is it that security is considered to be 'problematical' as a public good, and what justification might there be for suggesting that security cannot be a constitutional public good? It will soon become apparent that taking 'security' as the basis of a more detailed study will reveal much more about the more general distinction I made between 'public goods' as being understood either instrumentally and constitutionally. I expect the study of the good of security will reveal, in much greater depth, what is meant by 'instrumentalism' and in so doing will lay appropriate foundations for a more detailed consideration as to how the distinction between instrumentalism and constitutionalism becomes integral to understanding the practices of the AFSJ. In so doing the relationship also becomes significant in so far as it implicates our understanding of the EU as a political community.

The first part of this chapter explores the paradoxical nature of security as a public good. It becomes apparent that security suggests itself as close to the most foundational questions of constitutional life: the very sense that our common commitments must be *secured* and that, moreover, the political community itself must have *security* seems to mark it out as the foundational requirement of collective existence. However, in so far as we place security in such importance, as a constitutional commitment, we paradoxically risk neglecting to think of its constitutional dimensions. Instead, what becomes dominant in our way of thinking about security is to seek the means of its realisation in terms of the satisfaction of the most primary collective need. It is this rather peculiar position of security, as what I shall call the 'super public good', that means that it is appropriate to accord it particular scrutiny. The position of security as being able to intensify *both* our understanding of common commitment to a political community but also to be employed instrumentally, as a mode of delivering a fundamental need, becomes particularly apparent in the context of the AFSJ, and the wider EU, due to the contested nature of the site of political community for the EU (a matter which we explored at some length in Chapter 1). In attempting to develop this understanding of security as the pivotal public good it becomes important to explore the relationship between security and the practices which tend towards instrumentalism – I shall call such practices 'governmental'.[1] In the course of this chapter I shall refer to the work of Michel Foucault who has explored, in some considerable depth, the extent to which 'security' has emerged as a technique of governance, and particularly how it has become crucial to establishing control over claims to space, or area, and population. It will become apparent that the 'problem' of security is one which has emerged as an instrumental apparatus of government rather than being thought about (additionally) in a constitutional sense. This last point must be heavily underscored as it captures the progression from our development of the idea of constitutional legitimacy, as a distinctive deliberation about the collective commitments of a political community, in the previous two chapters, to the consideration of the practices of the AFSJ. In short, it becomes central to this argument that the mode of thinking which we can broadly call constitutionalism is different from the practices of 'governmentality' – and the recognition of such a distinction becomes central if we are to reserve the sense in which security can be understood as a constitutional public good.

The first part of this chapter provides the appropriate background to an examination of the attempt to recover a constitutional understanding of security, and, in particular, the important contribution by Loader and Walker in their book *Civilising Security*. Loader and Walker's project of recovering security as the basis for political trust and solidarity is principally directed, in addition, to the resurrection of the state as the security 'provider'. This is an indication of the extent to which the fortunes of both security and the state have become intertwined. However, it is clear that the concerns about the relationship between security and governmental practices also manifests in a more general sense and certainly bears upon the emerging practices of the AFSJ. In that sense I support the overall conclusions of Loader and Walker's work; that security can be capable of supporting genuinely constitutional political practices. However, I do not share their understanding of individual participation or involvement on the basis of which security is constituted as a public good. Ultimately Loader and Walker explain the capacity for security to be a 'public good', in the sense of providing political trust, by locating the 'reflexive' agency of individuals to cope with risks by 'putting their common security needs in common'. I intend to subject their understanding of 'reflexivity' to scrutiny, particularly in so far as it is adequate to overcome the difficulties as to how 'security' has become intertwined with governmental practices.

The overall direction of this chapter is to deepen our understanding of the problems of instrumentalism by taking the example of security, which has emerged as a powerful 'technique of governmentality'. This chapter sets out to explore the parameters of what I mean by techniques of 'governmentality', in relation to the good of security, and also to reinforce the importance of

1 And the corresponding term – 'governmentality'.

constitutionalism as a basis for rethinking our understanding of security in the practices of common political life.

Security and Techniques of Governing

Whilst 'instrumental' public goods are a necessary component of political activity it is the extent to which security has become the 'super-good', the ultimate felt need which collective life must deliver and which forms the fundamental basis for any common political commitment, which is beginning to attract scrutiny. There is now a considerable sociological and social theory literature based around the study of security which testifies to the preponderance of such practices both politically and socially. Although a review of such literature is beyond the scope of this book, I do want to indicate certain approaches as a preparation for a consideration of 'governmentality'.

It has become common place to understand 'security' as the fundamental basis upon which our collective life is governed. There is a visible infrastructure of security with which we must negotiate in both our public and private lives. Most of us are all too familiar with the ever-increasing demands of such security infrastructure upon the way we travel, work and enjoy pastimes. However, as well as this material manifestation of security, there is also the psychological or subjective perception of security; the sense that there are unprecedented threats that are generated by the various aspects of modern life.[2] It is perhaps the unknown aspect to such threats that leads to an overwhelming individual, and also collective, anxiety about the risks and dangers to be faced. Such anxiety is accompanied by the often obsessive searching and striving that is undertaken to ensure an adequacy of preparation and response so as to maintain risks within perceived acceptable levels. In such circumstances it is, perhaps, unsurprising that security seems to elude clarity not only concerning the nature of the risks or threats that we face but also the sorts of collective needs and interests to which it refers. As Zedner considers, in her book *Security*, what is most striking about the word 'security' is that it denotes a 'promiscuous concept ... appearing as different objects of desire in different places and at different times'.[3]

That security has developed as a concept which we deploy in a variety of different ways, and circumstances, has become the focus of attention for International Relations. The area of research known as 'security studies' was developed primarily by a group at the Copenhagen Institute, most notably Barry Buzan and Ole Wæver in the early 1990s (the end of the Cold War).[4] The thrust

---

2 Lucia Zedner, *Security* (London: Routledge, 2009) at p. 17.

3 Lucia Zedner, ibid., p. 9.

4 See in particular their seminal work: Ole Wæver, Barry Buzan, Morten Kelstrup and Pierre Lemaitre, *Identity, Migration and the New Security Agenda in Europe* (London: Pinter, 1993).

of their work is that security cannot be objectively defined or determined but is understood as emerging from the speech acts that we deploy. The research of the Copenhagen School has allowed the term security to be shifted into new areas, or sectors as they call it, including:

- the 'political', where the legitimacy of a governmental authority is challenged by relevant ideological threats;
- the 'societal', in which the identity of the social group becomes unstable due to cultural flows, population movements or economic activity; and
- the 'environmental' sector, where the social group is challenged by conditions of persistent pollution, land cultivation difficulties or denigration of the natural world by industrial activity.[5]

According to the exponents of 'security studies' what elevates a matter, in one of these sectors, into a security threat is a speech act which calls for extraordinary measures which suspend, or displace, the routines and norms of everyday politics. It is argued, therefore, that by claiming that existential threats are triggered this lifts them beyond ordinary politics as a security issue, and an agent claims a justification to treat them by extraordinary means.[6] However, any assertion of a security issue would have to be successfully accepted by the relevant audience and conform to the relevant rhetorical or linguistic conventions.[7] What becomes particularly interesting in the work carried out by security studies is the relationship between security and the political and legal order; whereby security seems to become the authority upon which the political–legal order is founded.[8] This conception of securitization does, if nothing else, offer a sense that securitization may lead to a circumstance whereby the public good of security has become the only basis for constitutional legitimacy, a most troubling viewpoint. Whether we will ever be confronted by this circumstance can only be a matter of conjecture at present.

Even if we are yet to be able to adopt such an absolute point concerning the relationship between the political order and security, the work of security studies does point to trends that ought to be taken into consideration. The expansion of security into new 'sectors', by semantic usage, does presuppose that security is

5 See Barry Buzan, *People, States and Fear: An Agenda for International Security Studies in the Post-Cold War Era* (London: Harvester Wheatsheaf, 1991). There has also been mooted the possibility of a religious sector.

6 Barry Buzan, Ole Wæver and Jaap de Wilde, *Security: A New Framework for Analysis* (Boulder, CO): Lynne Rienner, 1998), p. 26.

7 Ibid., p. 32. Of course this therefore makes the theory subject to probability or predictability theories, since there is a set of objective structural criteria (or what Austin and Wittgenstein might refer to as language conventions) which allow us to determine what sort of speech acts are likely to be effective and so on.

8 Michael C. Williams, 'Words, Images, Enemies: Securitization and International Politics', 47 *International Studies Quarterly* (2003), pp. 511–531.

a word that is used as a mode of expressing something about the way of things over which we aim to control, or that which we need or desire. A different way of phrasing this would be that 'security' is emerging as a 'super-good'; the primary justification as to how we organise our governmental practices to deliver needs, interests or results (whether or not this is in fact achievable and can be satisfied). Even if it can be accepted that 'security' is becoming shorthand for the ultimate achievements, aspirations or even the deepest fears of governance, what is unclear is the effects that this has on the way in which we experience this form of security governance. This emerges as the critical issue for this chapter: can security be a source of political commitment as opposed to an over-arching instrumental good to be pursued?

On the basis of what has already been written it becomes quite plausible to presume that the expansion in the term security and the accompanying techniques and procedures of security in contemporary lives must be a matter which is comparatively recent, or at least has only become apparent in its current form as 'super-good' reasonably recently. However, the expansion of the term security as *the* technique of government was the concern of Michel Foucault, in the 1970s and 1980s, and he sought to demonstrate how security emerged as one of the foremost techniques of government, the practices of which are deeply rooted in the development of the state. In the series of lectures that Foucault gave in 1978–79, which he called *Security, Territory and Population* he referred to these developing procedures, techniques and apparatus of control, by the state, as the 'technologies of security'. For an understanding as to the deep underlying aspects of how security has become a mode of instrumentalism which conceals or enables us to neglect its aspect as a constitutional public good, it is important to consider Foucault's work on the technologies of security in some detail.

Central to the development of Foucault's ideas concerning the technologies of security is the word *conduire* as an indication of the activity of governing, which becomes the term 'conduct of conduct'. As Mitchell Dean remarks, *conduire* can be understood in many forms as a verb (the act of directing or driving); as a reflexive verb (to conduct oneself) or as a noun which indicates a definitive sort of behaviour (for example, 'professional conduct').[9] The various ways in which the term *conduire* can be understood allows Foucault to offer a subtle sense of government as the *conduire* of human conduct. What is marked out by Foucault for particular attention is the means by which this conduct of human affairs has become particularly synonymous with techniques and technologies by which the architecture of spaces and the needs of a population can be shaped in such a way as to service the overall social goals of the economy as the emerging power base of the modern state. What becomes a particular interest, for Foucault, is the technique of directing the needs and biological processes of a population (bio-power) and this becomes of fundamental significance to the development of technologies of

9 Mitchell Dean, *Governmentality: Power and Rule in Modern Society* (London: Sage, 2010).

security; '[the genesis] of a political knowledge that put the notion of population and the mechanisms for ensuring its regulation at the center of its concerns'.[10]

What constitutes the genesis of the conduct of the needs of a population is in fact one of the central questions of *Security, Territory and Population.* Foucault traces the history of this activity to the pastoral power that emerged in the ancient East, and was then introduced to the West by the ecclesiastical powers of the institutionalised Christian (Latin) Church. The theme of pastoral power lies in the control that a shepherd has over his flock; the shepherd does not control a territory but a multitude moving towards a goal (either expressly identified or assumed). The shepherd is responsible for the welfare and the care of the flock and is prepared to accord as much value to a single sheep as the whole flock (that is, the flock is recognised to consist of individuals). The shepherd is also prepared to sacrifice himself for the welfare of the flock.[11] Interestingly, Foucault remarks that in Greek and Roman cultures, whilst there was knowledge of the pastoral-ruler there was not, it seems, the possibility of a 'government' which sought to conduct individuals throughout their lives by putting them under an authority of a guide who is responsible for what they do and what happens to them.[12]

The origins of the pastoral, in its Christian heritage, where the salvation of the soul from sin was the reason for the care provided by the shepherd over his flock, becomes transformed in the early modern period. With the early modern period the objective to be sought was not everlasting salvation but economic production and the 'soul' of man becomes 'biological' man as a member of a surplus (labouring) population. The technologies, and the consequent control over the population, therefore, radically alter the understanding of government. The transition is from the traditional virtues of the shepherd: wisdom, justice, respect for divine laws and the common skills (prudence, reflected decisions, care over oneself) to an 'art' of governance that finds the principles of its rationality and the specific domain of its application in the 'State'. Foucault terms this transformation 'governmentality' and exemplifies this by the use of *Polizeiwissenschaft*, 'the theory and analysis of everything that tends to affirm and increase the power of the state, to make good use of its forces, to procure the happiness of its subjects and chiefly the maintenance of order and discipline, the regulations that tend to make life convenient and provide them with the things they need to live'.[13]

Foucault's work locates the problem of security as an apparatus of governing, of exercising control over a population; a practice which has been taking place over a long period of time and, therefore, forms part of a deeply held understanding of modern government. Foucault seems to present the issue of 'governmentality'

---

10 Michel Foucault, *Security, Territory, Population* (London: Palgrave Macmillan, 2004), at p. 363.

11 Ibid., p. 129.

12 With the exception of certain specified relationships: doctor, gymnastics master and teacher.

13 Michel Foucault, *Security, Territory, Population*, at p. 366.

as the primary experience of political life in modern states. So much so, that we might understand 'governmentality' as the replacement of a constitutional life with an increasingly technological application of the pastoral power. Indeed, this is what seems most disturbing about Foucault's work – the technologies of security are presented as an all-encompassing mode of control over populations, offering to care or nurture their biological needs, interests or desires in so far as this tends towards their economic goals. What remains conspicuous in its absence is the notion that the multitude, or population, are participants in guiding the exercise of the techniques of control; or, perhaps, can even offer some resistance to it. I am not certain that there is a direct response to be found in Foucault's lectures on *Security, Territory and Population* but it is suggestive that Foucault's work does shift, in the early 1980s, and the question over the 'care of the self' or '*le souci de soi*' marked a consideration of new modes of subjectivity and relational ways of living, where such efforts may provide means of resisting the techniques of governmentality in the modern state.[14]

The understanding of 'governmentality' that emerges does not seem to encompass that kind of public meaning, and its related freedom, that we explored in the previous chapter when considering constitutional public goods. In fact it would seem that the 'technologies of security', as exhibited by the state, precisely exclude thinking about involvement with constitutional life and the spaces where the public meaning of goods can be constituted. Foucault's work presents us with this dilemma: security becomes a 'good' that displays an overwhelming degree of instrumentality and seeks to conduct every aspect of how our lives are governed, but by becoming the dominant mode of political strategy it fundamentally destabilises politics itself by undermining the possibility of thinking about the *public* good. It is the argument adopted by this book that constitutionalism is a mode of thinking about collective life which remains distinct from the techniques of 'governmentality'. However, the problem is whether security can be invoked as part of the language of constitutionalism and therefore as a limit on the techniques of governmentality or whether it will always lie outside and become a way of neglecting to think about constitutional life.

The destabilising effects of security, in so far as it relates to constitutional life, become more apparent when the question is posed: where do the political practices associated with the provision of security take place? Recent research, in the field of criminology, has traced 'new distributions'[15] of security whereby the distinctive public space of the state takes on an ambivalent character. The rise of 'security' as a commodity, to be provided by the market through networks of private firms and entrepreneurial security experts, has proliferated, but in a paradoxical sense, according to criminologists, this has also amplified the criminal justice state. The demand for security against threats has increased the demands upon the state to take punitive action and equally the regulation and supervision of

14 Michel Foucault, *The Hermeneutics of the Subject* (New York: Picador, 2004).

15 Lucia Zedner, *Security*, p. 49.

private security firms (agencies) has provided new layers of activity for the state.[16] Nevertheless even if the security technologies of the state have developed and deepened, as a result of the privatisation of security, it is also true that the state, as the site for the inter-relation between security and governmentality, can be seen as an episode in such a development. The study that we are embarked upon, with the AFSJ, demonstrates how security has also shifted to political practices which no longer exclusively refer to the state as *the* exclusive location for the provision of security.[17] Here we potentially encounter the paradox of security in its fullest sense: the need to deliver security becomes more paramount than the political life which must under-gird its own meaning. In the context of the EU this becomes most acute where security is compelled to become the primary sense in which we understand our political activity as the very activity of constituting a community.

Contemporary studies in criminology enhance our understanding as to the ways that the security discourse reinforces the dominance of instrumental forms of government. Zedner has commented upon the highly paradoxical nature of security; if we think that more security will lead to better political forms then this is wrong because 'security' treated as an unqualified public good paradoxically undermines itself. The pursuit of security leads to deeper anxiety, restrictions on freedom and in general seems to destabilise our very sense of 'public', understood as the civic trust which is a prerequisite of the common political life.[18]

Before considering the possibilities for constitutional thought faced with the 'problem' of security as a good I would like to try to summarise this section and also bring us back to the particular issues confronting the EU's 'area of freedom, security and justice'. We have remarked that one of the principal concerns about security as a 'public good' is that it would seem to undermine, in quite a paradoxical sense, the importance given to public meaning (in the sense that I have discussed this phrase in earlier passages of the book). Instead, following a reading of Michel Foucault's work, security is presented as an apparatus of control or care over a population. In the European context, in which we have seen a claim to represent the security concerns, the difficulty emerges over whether the AFSJ can sustain a public meaning of security sufficient to support its own policy goals and aspirations in respect of internal security. I intend to take up this question, in more detail, in the next chapter as we explore some of the specific practices of the AFSJ. However, at this point, it highlights something crucial from the foregoing analysis: that treating security as a 'public good' has implications for our sense of political agency; our involvement in constitutional life. This is particularly so in

16 Ibid., pp. 145–146.

17 See the earlier discussion of this point in Chapter 1 above.

18 Lucia Zedner, 'Too much Security?', 31 *International Journal of the Sociology of Law* (2003), pp. 155–184, see pp. 157–173, and *Technologies of Insecurity: Surveillance and Security of Everyday Life* (London: Routledge, 2008).

the EU because whilst we may be presented with common security practices the notion of a constitutional life is particularly contentious.[19]

Security as a 'Constitutional Public Good'?

The previous section presented the problems associated with conceiving security as a constitutional public good. Nevertheless, there is some suggestion that security might be responsive to constitutional considerations such as fairness, equality and basic political liberties.[20] However, the deeper issue concerning the relationship between security and governance concerns how, and whether it is possible, to understand security as a facet of our experience of a constitutional life. An important contribution to this debate comes from the work of Ian Loader and Neil Walker in *Civilizing Security*.[21] In offering an account of *Civilizing Security* I would like to draw us back to the question of the distinctive agency involved in revealing the meaning of constitutional public goods, a matter that was pursued in the last sections of the previous chapter.

The question asked in *Civilizing Security* is whether it is possible to realise conditions of political trust and solidarity. The beginning of a response to this question is that there is a social element to security; because security is not something that can be conceived entirely as a private response but rather is intimately and inexorably related to our social lives. This, therefore, is the foundation stone for the search for a civilised notion of security: how do we understand the social preconditions of security, that is to say, how is it that security becomes meaningful for us in a social context? Loader and Walker answer this by suggesting that there are two social preconditions of security: the inter-subjective security situation and the subjective element. The inter-subjective involves:

> [the] relationship between the catalogue of person and property securing measures in place to protect the individual, on the one hand, and the propensity of third parties to threaten that individual's security interests, notwithstanding the catalogue of protection, on the other.[22]

---

19 Hans Lindahl, 'European Integration: Popular Sovereignty and a Politics of Boundaries', 6 *European Law Journal* (2000), pp. 239–256.

20 'more generally, security policies should be judged according to principles of *fairness* (that is, they should not burden sub-groups or individuals unduly) and of *equality* ... And in the light of our earlier argument about the need for security measures to conduce to the ends sought, they should also be rights-regarding, and insofar as is possible therefore consistent with such basic civil liberties as freedom of movement, freedom of expression and individual privacy', Lucia Zedner, *Security*, pp. 172–173.

21 Ian Loader and Neil Walker, *Civilizing Security* (Cambridge: Cambridge University Press, 2007).

22 Loader and Walker, *Civilizing Security*, at p. 155.

The inter-subjective element of security depends upon the attitude or actions of others in providing the sorts of protective measures that ensure the protection of the individual. So, for instance, the co-operation of public security officials and others; including commercial security officials, friends, neighbours or other concerned citizens. What is advanced here is that the material aspects of security presuppose a high degree of social co-operation and co-ordination amongst various sorts of private and public actors.

The second social precondition of security, the subjective element, emerges from the realisation that the good of security is a product of the social condition that is '*in*security'. Loader and Walker suggest that:

> [S]ecurity refers not only to the provision of the objective measures of safety put in place in the form of police officers, crime prevention equipment, a safety-aware built environment, etc., at the level of 'problem-solution' but also, and more fundamentally, to those risks and dangers that are inherent in and the product of the social environment.[23]

Attention is drawn to the issue that a person's sense of security is not solely dependent upon the material or objective features of security sustained by others but about how these are experienced or interpreted by the individual: 'the socially inflected experience of feeling or not feeling secure is itself internal to and partially constitutive of what we mean by insecurity'.[24] This 'subjective' component becomes important to the scheme developed by Loader and Walker, and seems to provide a way of understanding that civilizing security is about ensuring that individuals are able to cope with the socially generated forms of insecurity: 'the overall measure of an individual's sense of security is the extent to which that individual feels free of *anxiety* about the existence, extent and stable reproduction of the objective or inter-subjective conditions of his or her security'.[25]

It is in these building blocks, regarding the social features of security, that it is possible to appreciate the direction of their work. The social or public good of security is about ensuring that individuals can cope, or can feel at ease, with the knowledge that their personal sense of security, and therefore also insecurity, emerges from the social. Granting this, the next question would be how are we to cope or feel at ease with the social meanings generated by security?

Loader and Walker respond to this issue by presenting two fundamental ideas, 'reflexivity' and the 'constitutive'. Let us take the notion of the 'constitutive' first. The functional benefits derived from resolving the practical features of our security condition are not a sufficient glue to ensure an ethical participation or involvement in the reproduction of our social meanings. Put simply, developing stable and civilised social meanings of security cannot be premised on ever more

23 Ibid., p. 156.

24 Loader and Walker, *Civilizing Security*, at p. 157.

25 Ibid., p. 158.

advanced technologies or infrastructures. For example, it does not make sense to say that if we place a CCTV camera on every street we will feel more secure; instead, we must seek a non-instrumental or non-technical explanation for stable and lasting societal security. I would agree with Loader and Walker that the only feasible explanation for robust social meanings comes down to finding common meanings of security: 'it [security] must therefore be predicated upon a set of actual or projected ends *as* common ends…'.[26] Importantly the realisation or aspiration of security is bound up with the identification of a political community as being a felt 'sense of common publicness', just in the manner that territory and common language may also be factors in social identification.[27] This is what was meant by the 'constitutive' dimension.

At this point we might ask whether Loader and Walker reify the collective or social dimension to the point that this deprives our agency or responsibility to forge collective meaning in some way. Whilst there is no doubt that Loader and Walker are seeking a more public sense of what security might mean I do not think that they can be guilty of advocating such a conception of security as a public good which excludes a sense of political agency on the part of the individual. The authors draw a distinction between a value that is perceived as emanating from the very fact of sharing, in other words the 'thickest' conception of the public goods, and goods that are valued because we come to understand them as needing to be shared. This distinction reintroduces the notion of human agency because it is our *recognition* of what is valuable about the good of security as socially shared that constitutes its (collective) meaning. It is this 'recognition' that Loader and Walker describe as the 'reflexive' dimension of security as a public good. Consider, for instance, the following passage:

> For what the constitutive dimension introduces, crucially, is an idea of reflexivity. It pinpoints how and why social collectivities, given the inextricability of collective purpose and social sense of self and the centrality of the idea of common security in the forging of that inextricable link, come to think of themselves and sustain thinking of themselves as social collectivities, such that they possess and may further pursue a common sense of and collective commitment to security and to various other collective-commitment-presupposing and identity-vindicating common goods … Security, in this adjusted perspective, is irreducibly social not in the sense that the good lies exclusively in the fact of sharing but in that, alongside its objective and individuated conditions of achievement, it nevertheless provides an example of goods that essentially incorporate common understandings of their value. *This is to say, our capacity to reach some level of common understanding and recognition of the terms of our collective security is itself a contributory factor in that collective security.*[28]

26 Ibid., p. 163.

27 Loader and Walker, *Civilizing Security*, at p. 164.

28 Ibid., p. 164. The authors' emphasis.

Fundamentally it is through reflexivity that we learn to cope with the feelings of security and insecurity that come from our social lives. It is in this sort of 'social learning' where we master our own feelings and where 'security is understood and configured not as a perpetual form of striving, but as a state of well *being* – a state in which we are able to live – and live together – securely with risk'.[29] Hence, security as a public good, in the constitutional sense, is understood as mastering our feelings about the risks and contingencies of living in a political community, which, as Loader and Walker suggest, is part and parcel of our social identification (our collective being). The strength of Loader and Walker's work, from a constitutional perspective, is in this attempt to link security as a constitutive good with re-configuring a notion of the 'subject' of social/political life and, consequently, the nature of participation or involvement in such practices. It is this fundamental aspect of how must begin to think about the dimensions of political trust of security which is addressed by the notion of reflexivity.

The basis of my own argument differs in respect of the understanding of political involvement or agency conveyed by the term 'reflexivity'. The understanding that is developed by Loader and Walker concerning 'reflexivity' is not robust enough to be able to offer a view of security that is a source of political commitment, or, in the terms that we have been developing in this chapter, capable of resisting the technologies of security. In making this argument it becomes necessary to draw upon the arguments of previous chapters concerning the distinctive deliberation of constitutionalism and the sense of individual agency in being a participant in the meaning of constitutional public goods.

'Reflexivity' owes its contemporary currency to the attempts to understand how individuals can cope and develop reflexive practices in order to be able to meet the changing and dynamic demands of modernization. The social theorist, Ulrich Beck, has become one of the principal advocates of the notion of 'reflexive modernization' and explores ways of thinking about, and adapting to, the structural changes of the 'risk society' in which out of the post-industrial age society undermines and undercuts its own foundations for control.[30] The two features with respect to this lack of control are firstly where threats are systematically produced but do not become public issues or the centre of political conflicts and, secondly, even when risks produced do become part of the political debate, the industrial society becomes the manufacturer of threats that cannot be controlled.[31] Beck's aim is to ensure that politics emerges in such a way as to allow individuals, and groups,

29 Ibid., p. 169.

30 Ulrich Beck, *Risk Society: Towards a New Modernity* (London: Sage, 1992) and Ulrich Beck, Anthony Giddens and Scott Lash, *Reflexive Modernization: Politics, Tradition and Aesthetics in the Modern Social Order*.

31 In part, Beck argues that such risks follow from the nature of instrumental rationality that is seen as all-pervasive in risk societies. For instance he writes that risk issues cannot be issues of order, instead 'they are the form in which the instrumentally rational logic of control and order leads itself by virtue of its own dynamism ad absurdium', ibid., p. 10.

to come to terms with the difficulties of living in a post-industrial risk society.[32] Towards this end, Beck conceives of reflexivity as a form of self confrontation concerning the effects of the risk society on the way we live our lives.[33] The theme developed by Beck is that the peculiar age of change and risk that we live in requires a confrontation of the self in order to build up the emotional resilience to ensure that a robust and adaptable form of 'new politics' emerges.

Anthony Giddens also argues that reflexivity is important for the building of emotional or psychological resources of the individual in order to come to terms with the flux of modernity. In his seminal work, *The Constitution of Society*,[34] Giddens develops a sense of the human agent which is linked to this ability to cope with the social world. His thesis is that the self is not solely dependent upon psychological mechanisms; within the personality of the individual actor they also become mediated by social processes which individuals sustain by the routine practices of their daily lives.[35] We learn this from the very earliest experiences of childhood, whereby engagement with others depends upon routines of stabilised social behaviour that engender trust.[36]

Giddens recognises that the kind of modernisation described by Beck places huge pressures on the idea of agency grounded in stable routines and describes the idea that we seem to be part of an experiment without control:

> we are all caught up in a grand experiment, which is at the one time our doing – as human agents – yet to an imponderable degree outside our control. It is not an experiment in the laboratory sense, because we do not govern the outcomes within fixed parameters, it is more like a dangerous adventure.[37]

Giddens writes that reflexivity offers a therapy for our 'collective addictions'; this involves an 'excavation of the past'[38] as a means of becoming more emotionally

---

32 See the distinction he draws between rule-altering politics and rule-directed politics, and the importance of the emergence of sub-political groups and organisations on p. 37. He may be right about the emergence of 'new politics', but I do not see that it necessarily must follow the way he has set it out.

33 Ibid., p. 6.

34 Anthony Giddens, *The Constitution of Society: An Outline of a Theory of Structuration* (Cambridge: Polity Press, 1984).

35 Ibid., p. 50.

36 See the following quote, 'The mother is an agent (already a representative of the generalized other) who in caring for the infant, lays a social claim upon it that presages the normative sanctions associated with the later formation of social relationships. The anxiety of absence is defused through the engagement and disengagement on which the diversity of encounters is based', ibid., p. 54.

37 Ulrich Beck, Anthony Giddens and Scott Lash, *Reflexive Modernization*, p. 58.

38 Consider the following quote which reveals the metaphor he uses to convey this notion of the uncovering the past in order to overcome it: 'So far as the post-traditional society is concerned, what is interesting is what I shall call the process of excavation

confident about modernity, in which we are not guided or supported by formulaic truths or customs but rather make choices for which we have complete authorship. Hence modernisation, as well as causing difficulties of coping or emotional stability, is also to be celebrated as heralding an age of unparalleled possibility and freedom to choose and live lives that our forebears could not have entertained.[39]

This understanding of 'reflexivity' as an emotional coping with social life, and possibly our shifting expectations about the goods that we seek to secure for ourselves, and others, resonates with the understanding used by Loader and Walker that 'reflexivity' is a mode of living securely with the risks generated in society. Whilst this suggests that we become aware of the psychological dimensions of our social lives, and therefore to appreciate the consequences of emotional harm as a result of shifting perception of risk, I do not think it is capable of accounting for the distinctive involvement in constituting security as the basis for a political trust or commitment.

Implicit in the understanding of reflexivity is a certain notion of engagement with social practices. Reflexivity, in the sense used by Loader and Walker, involves the recognition by the subject that the practices of security, and the sources of risk, are inherently social. On the basis of this recognition it becomes possible for the subject to be able to live securely with this risk because the conditions of his or her own security are premised around generating shared trust in the provision of security. Underlying this approach, therefore, is the idea that the subject can make the social practices of security into an object of understanding – the goal of which is to understand it as having a necessary social precondition.

The first potential difficulty concerns whether it is possible for reflexivity to be a means of overcoming the practices of security so as to recognise what makes it a precondition of political trust. The practices of security, which we explored in the previous section, in fact do present a strong sense in which security can be a mode of political trust, but one which sees this primarily through the lens of the technical goals and needs of a population in pursuit of economic goods. The risk is that reflexivity rather than providing a different mode of understanding, and therefore expressing, the political trust of security merely reinforces the view of security as instrumental by requiring that the social perception of risk can be met by the conduct of politics. Another way of putting this is to say that what reflexivity achieves is a way of knowing what feelings of risk remain unacknowledged by the technical apparatus of security and so invite an instrumental response. In so far as reflexivity implies making the practices of political life a basis for assessing the extent to which one's subjective anxiety or need are fulfilled then it remains difficult to escape from the understanding of security as an instrumental public

---

involved. Excavation, as in an archaeological dig, is an investigation, and it is also an evacuation. Old bones are disinterred, and their connections with one another established, but they are also exhumed and the site cleaned out. Excavation means digging deep, in an attempt to clean out the debris of the past', ibid., p. 72.

39 Ibid., pp. 73–74.

good. Related to this is the sense that reflexivity will not be able to counter, and may well reinforce, the atavistic impulse to accept arbitrary risk so long as its impact is not directly to undermine the conditions of security enjoyed by an élite.

The deeper problem is that it is ingrained that we expect that constitutional life *will be* able to relieve us of anxiety and consequently provide security. Counter to this I would claim that in fact, it becomes a condition of constitutional life that we cannot necessarily expect this to be delivered – or at least our participation can only be premised on the basis that our common constitutional commitments, including that of security, are inherently good and not because they can be made to assuage anxiety, a sense of risk or other personal need. An illustration of the failure of reflexivity to indicate a mode of thinking about political trust is indicated in the following passage from Loader and Walker:

> the overall measure of an individual's sense of security is the extent to which the individual feels free of anxiety about the existence, extent and stable reproduction of the objective and inter-subjective conditions of his or her security.[40]

The problem posed by security is clearly conveyed by this sentence. Like Loader and Walker I would agree that we might describe security, in its constitutional sense, as when we are secure in our engagement, or participation, in constitutional life. However, as soon as we expect such an engagement to provide a means by which an individual 'feels free of anxiety' then it becomes understood as an instrumental public good. It is a fine distinction but ultimately a crucial one.

Conclusion

The difficulties of understanding security as a constitutional public good, as the basis for common commitments which are inherently valued, run very deep. The chapter began by noting that 'security' seems almost to have a dialectical structure, that whilst security becomes one of the most foundational needs of a political community it also undermines the conditions for the experience of a secure political community. Given this inherently paradoxical structure it is easy to understand why the conclusion is reached that security must be inimical to a political way of life. The extent to which our practices have tended to emphasise that security becomes the ultimate good (the super-good) by which the needs and welfare of a population must be met by the development of techniques and methods of governmental activity was encountered in the work of Michel Foucault. It becomes apparent that the term technologies of security refers to a deeply rooted set of practices in which the conduct of government acts upon the needs of a population in pursuit of economic power. This phenomenon Foucault terms 'governmentality'.

40 Loader and Walker, *Civilizing Security*, at p. 158.

The crucial question that emerges, from these studies, is whether it remains possible to think about security as a constitutional public good. I explored this question through the work of Loader and Walker, which took the view that it was possible to recover the sense in which security could be a basis for political trust and solidarity by recovering the extent to which our sense of risk and consequent need of security required recognition of the social components of these feelings. In this way security could become the basis of a common commitment as opposed to being inimical to public trust. Whilst sharing the normative direction of their work I also explored concerns about whether the central plank of their argument – the importance of 'reflexivity' – could remain robust enough to be able to ensure that we think about security as a basis for a common commitment. It is, perhaps, simply that it is just too ingrained that we think of security as an emotional need, or desire, which must be fulfilled or delivered by our constitutional life which prevents us from even being reflexive about this. It may be that in Loader and Walker's own project, which concerns the state as a provider of security, it is in fact not necessary to take an extra step away from the practices of the technologies of security – it is simply sufficient that security is to maintain its social preconditions as opposed to being provided wholesale by market forces. However, in terms of our current concerns, with the AFSJ, it seems that security is attempting to become the basis for thinking about the constitutional legitimacy of the EU as a political community, as the way in which we understand the EU as a political community. To this extent security *is* being asserted as *the* constitutional public good, and this presents us with the more difficult conundrum as the constitutional legitimacy of the practices of the AFSJ in large part rests upon the attempt to recover a mode of thinking which is different from the practices of governmentality.

Where does this leave us? It may seem that this chapter has not resolved the issue as to whether, and how, security can be conceived as a constitutional good. As I have already remarked, security must primarily be understood as a highly equivocal public good and liable to form part of the instrumental techniques of the conduct of government. However, in keeping with the trajectory of this book, any resistance to such practices must also be on the basis of a practical engagement in which an attempt is made to preserve, and understand, our common constitutional commitments. In this way it might be said that the issue is one of containment; that we ensure that the 'technologies of security' do not lead to conceiving other public goods as simply instrumental. Concern with this issue marks something of a change of approach, because what becomes important is to understand, on the basis of an interpretation of the current practices, the possibilities of practical action that are open. It certainly would be misleading to assume that the distinction between constitutional and instrumental public goods becomes a neat conceptual distinction in practice; instead reflection must become a way to attend to the practices themselves and the possibilities of construing them constitutionally. In this sense it worth recalling that the medium of our agency or involvement in constitutional public goods is the language and interpretive possibilities that a contrasting and rich vernacular of expression affords. Hence, a critical stance may be as straightforward as pointing out the necessary limitations of instrumental public goods; but it may also take the (related) form of augmenting the language of constitutional commitment to public goods in order to ensure that concerns over constitutional legitimacy and therefore the implied authority and shared existence of constitutional life can be expressed (those matters to do with thinking constitutionally that were addressed in Chapter 2). The next chapter begins to develop such a critical engagement with the practices of the AFSJ by exploring the extent to which the constitution of a space of free movement in the EU is radically limited by a view of security which seems to manifest many of the concerns raised in this chapter.

Chapter 5
The Construction of an *Area* of Freedom, Security and Justice: The Practices of Constitutional Life Examined

Introduction

Over the previous two chapters our efforts to highlight the issues of constitutional legitimacy coalesced around how to ensure a common commitment to freedom, security and justice as constitutional goods whilst recognising that such goods can be construed instrumentally. The last chapter reflected upon the problematical status of security as a good, which has evolved to occupy a close relationship with the development of practices of governmental control (governmentality). The recognition of the contentious nature of security, as a public good, establishes the problematic of constitutional legitimacy, of the AFSJ, in a clear way: given the already highly developed tradition of understanding security as related to governmentality how can the AFSJ (founded as it is on a commitment to security) hope to establish the constitutional commitments that, almost paradoxically, it craves? The response to this problem, if indeed we can think of it as a problem, does not lie in the theory or philosophy of constitutions, or politics, but instead in a practical engagement or concern with the AFSJ as a component of the constitutional life of the European Union. Nevertheless, reflection can also indicate the contours of a practice rather in the way that a map offers an indication of a terrain rather than a guide to a journey or even less an indication of the experience (meaning) of that journey. To this extent the next two chapters sketch the contours of the practice of constitutional life in the AFSJ, which will shape how we practically engage with the meaning of our commitment to the public goods of freedom, security and justice and offer an understanding of the place of the AFSJ as part of the constitutional authority of the EU.

This chapter focuses on the practices associated with the representation that the goods of freedom, security and justice are to be realised as an *area*. It is in this relationship, between public goods and a common or shared space, that important constitutional considerations are invoked. In particular, this chapter develops the insights of the previous chapter, in respect of the public good of security, to show the precarious 'balance' between instrumental understandings of public goods and constitutional public goods. The argument focuses on the relationship between free movement around the legally constituted area of the EU and the consequent security concerns or 'compensatory measures' adopted. It becomes apparent that the nature of these security measures is analogous to a technology of security. It is contended, through the study of the various policy documents, that the effect of these practices of security is to neglect the constitutional aspect of legal space in which a political people relate to space by their common commitments. It is this neglect which poses challenges for how we go about practically resolving the constitutional legitimacy of the current practices of the AFSJ.

The Area of Constitutional Involvement

Contained in the Treaty on the Functioning of the European Union is the assertion that 'the Union shall constitute an area of freedom, security and justice with respect for fundamental rights and the different legal systems and traditions of the Member States'.[1] Whilst the reference to an '*area*' may seem to be an innocuous one it deserves further reflection since it implies something of interest: that the EU is to be a place or space which can be identified with particular values, or practices, of freedom, security and justice. In fact, an 'area' suggests that the recognition of public goods as constitutional can only be done in so far as there is also a claim to an 'area'. However, it is not being unduly naive to ask what exactly it might mean to make such a reference to an 'area'. For example, does it mean that we attempt to refer to an actual space – is it a geographical area? Patrick Twomey writes, in the immediate aftermath of the Amsterdam Treaty, which established the AFSJ, that the rhetoric of a space where certain important values are fostered and protected becomes an attempt to construct the symbols or ideology of a territorial claim.[2] Certainly it is familiar, from the traditional understanding of state sovereignty within the doctrines of public international law, that an important feature of *de jure* political authority is the *de facto* control over territory. However, as we have already explored, in previous chapters, the relationship between the authority of the EU and traditional understandings of state sovereignty are problematical such that an uncomplicated translation of 'area' as a claim to territorial unity becomes difficult to sustain. Furthermore, the EU is in any case an unstable geographical territory. In the last decade alone the EU has expanded its borders all the way to Russia in the East and in the future expansion may incorporate Turkey,[3] which would mean that the EU's southern borders would stretch to Iran, thus according the EU an entirely different geo-political position. Given the shifting aspects of the geographical extent of the EU the reference to an 'area' does not, perhaps, intend to convey a claim concerning territorial boundary in such a straightforward sense.

1 Article 67 TFEU.

2 Patrick Twomey, 'Constructing a Secure Space: The Area of Freedom, Security and Justice' in *Legal Issues of the Amsterdam Treaty*, edited by David O'Keeffe and Patrick Twomey (Oxford: Hart Publishing, 1999), at p. 359.

3 Negotiations for Turkey's membership of the EU were started in 2005 but remain unresolved.

If we are not prepared to accept a straightforward reading of the word 'area', as denoting a territorial claim, then the understanding of Twomey seems to offer a more nuanced understanding of 'area'. If the reference to 'area' may be taken to be denoting the symbol, or ideology, of a territorial claim then the important follow-up question to this becomes: what is being 'symbolised' by such a claim to territory? The response appears to be clear; a representation of 'community', 'unity', or 'polity', in other words, 'area' refers to the political (collective) relationship to a space or place rather than simply the aspects of a physical landscape. Hans Lindahl conveys this mode of thinking, about place, when he writes about the AFSJ in the following manner:

> … legal place cannot be understood independently of collective identity. Legal communities are never simply located somewhere in space, like, say a boulder lying in a field. A community must – literally – find a place in a continuous process of relating to space, even in those comparatively recent cases, historically speaking, when its external borders are cartographically demarcated and stabilised. Indeed, a relation to an own place, hence a claim to territorial unity, is no less constitutive of sedentary communities, such as the nation-state or the EU, than it is of a nomadic community. In other words, what it means to be a community is to have to continuously re-interpret the claim to an own place.[4]

Central to this passage, and equally to the claim of 'area', is the role that law plays in establishing an 'own place' and he employs the term 'legal place' and 'legal communities' in order to indicate the crucial dimensions played by the law as means by which we relate to space in representing the 'ideology of territory'. In a later essay Lindahl provides some indication as to why law becomes important in assisting the way in which we relate to space:

> a legal space is a *space of action*, in contrast to, say, the space of perception. The law orders individual action by way of boundaries that establish where human behaviour ought or ought not to occur.[5]

The implication is that law establishes a unity by closing, or indeed separating, certain spaces (i.e. actions) as excluded; 'boundaries join by *separating*'.[6] Law constitutes this unity by positing normative boundaries that demarcate membership or involvement by ordering action. It is important to realise that Lindahl's argument actually relies upon two elements, that the structure of space

4 Hans Lindahl, 'Finding a Place for Freedom, Security and Justice: The European Union's Claim to Territorial Unity', 29 *European Law Review* (2004), at p. 465.

5 Hans Lindahl, 'Breaking Promises to Keep Them', in *A Right to Inclusion and Exclusion? Normative Fault Lines of the EU's Area of Freedom, Security and Justice* (Oxford: Hart Publishing, 2009), the author's emphasis.

6 Ibid., the author's emphasis.

created, or represented by the law involves: (i) a claim to common or collective interest (which he describes as forming a collective identity) and (ii) 'closing off an inside over an outside'.[7]

A claim to area or space is therefore a representation of collective commitments and to this extent it is possible to understand how this builds upon, or relates to, the previous work in respect of constitutional public goods. However, there is a second aspect to the claim to area and that is that such an *act* closes off space; it would seem that this implies a view that the boundaries or borders are determinable and fixed as a definitive *act* of the law. I would like to indicate how such a claim to area, as a way in which we use law to relate to space, becomes central to our concerns over constitutionalism throughout this book. The clue for this relationship comes with the word 'use' of law to create and support the claim to 'area' for in our 'use' of law we come up against the now familiar contrast between an instrumental understanding of collective life and a constitutional one. For instance, suppose it was asked what might be the consequences of an attempt to construct a legal space which did not have, to any significant degree, the component of collective commitment? In such a circumstance, we might think that the law simply closes off a space as a normative *act*, such as when a state claims a right of territorial control under public international law, or when a claim to territorial ownership is put forward by *imperium* or *dominium.*[8] In each case the legal space is simply an act of control or ownership which renders both the landscape and inhabitants as the subjects or property of the legally defined space. Therefore, a claim to territory, which lacks the element of collective interest, is an act of legal control, or use, which renders everything as an object to be defined by the law in terms of included or excluded (*jus includendi et excludendi*).[9]

Such a construction of legal space does have at least two important consequences. The first is that the boundary of the legal space tends to be viewed as non-relational, to the extent that without the element of commitment to a collective interest the legal space that is created does not become open-ended such that we can understand the task as being that 'a community [must] continuously re-interpret the claim to an own place'.[10] If legal boundaries are an act of relating to finding a place this becomes an uneasy and continuous task of interpretation and one that constitutes a community as a community. It is such a task of engagement which is concealed by the legal *act* of closing off a space. Secondly, if there is a fixed and determinate distinction between what is inside and outside the legal space then not only does this issue of membership of the community, as related to space, become a matter which is not subject to involvement (individuals are not related to space but subject to that space) but also tends to place an arbitrary exclusivity upon membership or make it subject to a specific (legal) criteria.

7 Ibid., p. 149.

8 Hans Lindahl, 'Breaking Promises to Keep Them', p. 145.

9 Ibid., p. 153.

10 Hans Lindahl, 'Finding a Place for Freedom, Security and Justice', at p. 465.

This chapter aims to trace the contours as to how instrumentalism develops in the legal practices which make a claim to represent the *area* of freedom, security and justice. In addition, I hope to be able to explore how this issue of the construction, and representation, of an *area* lies precisely on the fault line of our concerns over the constitutional legitimacy of the AFSJ. The basis of my argument is that the legal practices which establish the representation of 'area' in the AFSJ exhibit a tendency towards a legal closure of space which precludes the constitutional commitment underpinning an ongoing relationship to place in which common interests or public goods can be pursued. By treating the issue of the legal construction of space as crucial to the AFSJ it is possible to understand how precarious the balance is between an instrumental and a constitutional understanding of the public goods of freedom, security and justice. The representation of the *area* of freedom, security and justice is consequently a necessary part of understanding these goods as constitutional but this makes such goods, and the *area* itself, vulnerable to being understood entirely instrumentally. It will become apparent, in studying the legal practices of the AFSJ, that it is 'security' that plays a decisive role in the closure of legal space and therefore enables us to extend our understanding of the problems of security as a public good which we explored in the previous chapter.

Security at the Borders of Control

In this section we embark upon a consideration of the practices by which the law represents the public goods of security, freedom and justice as constituted inside a legal 'area'. I propose to explore the extent to which free movement of people, between the Member States, has become a means of establishing a strong legal control over the borders of the EU due to the way that free movement has become securitised through a variety of different practices. The intention is to try to explore the relationship between these different practices of security measures and freedom of movement by highlighting, and developing, the themes explored in the previous chapter about the precariousness of security as a constitutional public good. This discussion goes to the heart of concerns about constitutional legitimacy. My contention, in this chapter, is that it is possible to uncover an emerging trend whereby the construction of a legal area is completed by employing a highly instrumental notion of security and, in doing so, this risks undermining the necessary relationship between a common space and constitutional public goods and, consequently, our practical engagement in shaping the meaning of these constitutional goods. This failure to think about the constitutional dimension to our collective life, represented by the AFSJ, is also reinforced by the next chapter in which similar attitudes can be uncovered in relation to the legal practices of criminal law which aim to establish a common area of justice.

Let us first consider the relationship between free movement and this constitutional understanding of 'area'. The origin of the right of free movement around the EU, and the corresponding desire to abolish internal borders, came with the Single European Act of 1985, which in Article 8a stated that '[t]he internal market shall comprise an area without internal frontiers in which the free movement of goods, services, persons and capital is ensured in accordance with the provisions of the Treaty'. Despite the Treaty agreement which articulated the need, and political intention, to complete the economic freedoms of the internal market by an ambitious programme to abolish the internal borders, this policy was destined to commence life outside the Community legislation framework as an International Convention – Schengen.[11]

The Schengen Convention later became incorporated into the EU Treaty,[12] and it is possible to see that this document, and the various policies developed from it, forms an important basis of thinking about border control and freedom of movement in the EU. In particular, it is clear that the abolition of border controls is not just a question of realising a right to free movement in the EU, but also entails addressing important questions as to the security, law and order of the external borders of the EU. To this extent the regime of the abolition of internal border controls also contains measures concerning: harmonisation of visa policy; regulating the free movement of third country nationals between the signatories; further rules restricting irregular migration; allocating responsibility for asylum requests; addressing criminal judicial co-operation issues; and creating the database or the Schengen Information System (SIS). Echoing the views of others with regard to these measures, Steve Peers writes that, 'the underlying logic of the Schengen rules was that there must be extensive compensatory measures, including a common visa policy and transfer of checks to the external borders of the signatories, in order to ensure that internal border checks could be abolished without a loss of security'.[13] If we consider this quote more closely it offers two ways of thinking about the relationship between freedom of movement (border controls) and security; the first is that there is an inevitable interconnection between features associated with security and freedom of movement; and secondly that it is the 'compensatory measures' that become the principal focus of the legislative efforts regarding freedom of movement. It can be appreciated that the second implication of the quote is by far the more controversial and also in recent times (most clearly since 9/11) it has almost become a common assumption that the practices of freedom of movement risk being collapsed into security 'compensatory measures'. This becomes an important aspect of our inquiry; not only to demonstrate the nature of the security 'compensatory

11 This was first the 185 Schengen Agreement (also known as Schengen I) and then the 1990 Convention which implemented the agreement (Schengen II) see [2000] OJ L 239/13 and 19.

12 At Amsterdam in 1997; there was also the well-known issue of the opt-out of Ireland and the United Kingdom – which was negotiated and agreed to at Amsterdam.

13 Steve Peers, *EU Justice and Home Affairs Law* (Oxford: Oxford University Press, 2006), at p. 97.

measures' but to understand how the practice of such measures not only compels a certain understanding of security but equally affects the way in which we perceive a common area of free movement in the EU.[14]

It has already been narrated how, in the years following the Maastricht Treaty and then the Treaty of Amsterdam, the EU acquired greater institutional competence to legislate on matters of immigration, migration and border control. However, the decisive moment, in terms of the relationship between free movement and security, undoubtedly emerged in the aftermath of the terrorist attacks of 9/11. Steve Peers remarks that following the incorporation of the Schengen *acquis* into the EU treaty arrangements, the EC legal order suddenly acquired an extensive set of rules and procedures regarding border controls. In his view this explains the apathy in respect of developing new policy and proposals; 'it is striking that there was no reference to any measures on internal or external border in the Vienna plan and only a vague reference to operational cooperation in the Tampere Conclusions'.[15] But this apathy could not continue after the terrorist attacks in America on 9/11, when many European governments suddenly became highly concerned about their vulnerability to terrorism. In such a climate 'security' emerged as a political watchword, hence there seems to be a clear difference in the scope and depth of measures regarding the security dimension before and after 9/11.[16] It also seems to be the case that following 9/11 security measures, and our sense of risk, have appeared to be closely tied to events and the way in which different threats have become manifest. For example, we are all acutely aware of how our transit through airports changes in light of the current risks about security and possible attacks. However, in the course of this chapter, what is considered is an understanding of the deeper sense we have of security which is not so closely

14 Of course, it is also true that issues of free movement of persons in the EU also raise important questions regarding the provision of welfare and public services – as nationals and non-nationals move across borders. Whilst this is a very important aspect of free movement, it specifically raises matters that are to do with the internal market of the former first pillar regime, whereas here we are more expressly concerned with the relationship that develops between free movement and security: the AFSJ dimension. Nevertheless an interesting study of the relationship between free movement and welfare/economic goods can be found in Peiter van der Mei, *Free Movement of Persons within the European Community: Cross Border Access to Public Benefits* (Oxford: Hart Publishing, 2003).

15 Steve Peers, *Justice and Home Affairs*, p. 105. This is a reference to the European Council meetings that took place in Vienna (1998) and Tampere (1999).

16 Steve Peers states: 'however, the events of September the 11th, 2001 clearly changed the EU's priorities, with a perception that new visa and external control measures could enhance the objectives of increased security and control. A number of European Councils subsequently agreed policy objectives for this area with these objectives in mind', Ibid., p. 105. This view is also supported by Valsamis Mitsilegas, 'The Borders Paradox: The Surveillance of Movement in a Union without Internal Frontiers', in *A Right to Inclusion and Exclusion* edited by Hans Lindahl

bound to the daily sense of risk or threat but which touches upon the sense we have of it as instrumental or a constitutional public good.

In a study of the security measures in the EU following the 9/11 attacks, Michael Levi and David Wall suggest that a distinction must be drawn between what they call 'hard' and 'soft' security measures.[17] Hard security measures are those which seek to 'harden targets' and tend to take the form of measures intended to guard against physical intrusion or trespass, interference with funding opportunities and the protection of infrastructure (including information networks).[18] By contrast, soft security measures are those that, in the main, provide intelligence, and so become linked to the growing capability of surveillance technology. Soft security is said to reflect a shift to 'actuarial strategies' which rely upon targeted models of risk identification, the gathering of data surveillance and the analysis or specialist processing of data.[19] In a recent survey of the measures taken under free movement of people under the provisions of the AFSJ Mitsilegas confirms the increasing importance of technologies of 'soft security'. He identifies the following forms in which soft security measures have been developed in relation to border security: targeted risk identifications of suspected groups based on profiling; generalised collection and exchange of personal data (including biometrics) to different instances of movement across borders; and maximisation of data collection through the application to EU citizens and third country nationals.[20]

There are several examples of measures that indicate a definite trend towards 'compensatory security' with regard to free movement following 9/11, and these feature elements of both hard and soft security measures. By the end of 2001 the Council developed plans for an 'integrated borders management system' which was adopted in June 2002.[21] From this emerged several important proposals to be implemented. Firstly there was the creation of the European border agency, Frontex. Established under Council Regulation 2007/2004,[22] it was envisaged that Frontex would be responsible *inter alia* for 'coordination of operational cooperation between Member States in the field of external border control', 'research and information on external borders' and increasing 'technical and operational assistance'.[23] Now, it becomes quite apparent that this policy of

17 Michael Levi and David Wall, 'Technologies, Security, and Privacy in the Post-9/11 European Information Society', 31 *Journal of Law and Society* (2004), pp. 194–220 at p. 198.

18 Ibid., p. 199.

19 Ibid., p. 199.

20 See Mitsilegas, 'The Borders Paradox', p. 52.

21 See Council Document 100119/02, 'Plan for the management of the external borders of the Member States of the EU'; http://register.consilium.eu.int/pdf/en/02/st10/10019en2.pdf

22 Council Regulation, of 26 October 2004, 'Establishing a European Agency for the Management of Operational Cooperation at the External Borders of the Member States of the European Union', OJ L 349.

23 Ibid.

operational assistance and research and information is also developed through the creation and expansion of various databases, as part of the technology of security as surveillance. There is the reform and development of the Schengen Information System (termed SIS II);[24] a directive on the transmission of passenger data;[25] and also a Visa Information System (VIS).[26] The momentum towards technical and information systems as providing the basis for security is also evident in the new programme for the AFSJ, the Stockholm Action Plan (2010).[27] For example, the document presented by the Commission states a commitment to modern technologies:

> Smart use of modern technologies in border management to complement existing tools as part of a risk management process can also make Europe more accessible to bona fide travellers and stimulate innovation among EU industries, thus contributing to Europe's prosperity and growth, and ensure the feeling of security of Union's citizens. The coming into operation of the SIS II and VIS systems will be a high priority'.[28]

It is comparatively straightforward to identify measures and practices associated with movement of persons which provide for a security dimension in the techniques of surveillance and information technology employed. However, it is more significant to attempt to identify what might such practices mean, or indicate, in relation to our wider concerns about the way 'security' has become instrumental to constituting our very understanding of 'area'. The most appropriate place to start to look is the policy documents themselves which reveal an important indication of the potential meanings of these practices. One of the earliest efforts to annunciate the approach to be taken in respect of such security measures surrounding the issues of free movement was a document of the European Council called 'Plan for the Management of the External Borders of the Member States of the European Union' of 14 June 2002, in which the action plan for borders and security is developed. There is the assertion, very early on in the document, of the interconnection between the abolition of internal borders, through Schengen, and the importance of developing secure external borders: 'in an area like Schengen, characterised by the suppression of internal border

---

24 2001/886/JHA: Council Decision of 6 December 2001 on the development of the second generation Schengen Information System (SIS II) OJ L 328/4, and Council Regulation (EC) No 2424/2001 of 6 December 2001 on the development of the second generation Schengen Information System (SIS II) OJ L 328/4.

25 Directive, 'The obligation of carriers to communicate passenger data' [2004] OJ L 261/24.

26 Council Decision 2004/512/EC.

27 COM (2010) 171.

28 Ibid., p. 6.

controls, the surveillance and control of external borders is essential'.[29] It is to be noted that the main presupposition of what secure borders means is indicated by the term 'surveillance', in other words it is an operational oversight of the borders. This is made more explicit two paragraphs further on, 'This European Council conclusion calls attention to the fact that coherent, effective common management of the external borders of the Member States of the Union will boost security'.[30] This idea of the operational management of the borders eventually becomes, in para. 40, a five-point list of 'mutually interdependent components', which are: common operational coordination and cooperation mechanism; common integrated risk analysis; personnel and inter-operational equipment; common corpus of legislation; and burden-sharing between Member States and the Union. Hence it can be seen that the main presupposition of the action plan, devised by the European Council, contains a strong emphasis on the operational features of security. The next question is whether this is also carried over into the understanding of the specific measures themselves; and here it is worthwhile consulting the specific words of the Commission in the policy proposals released.

With this aim in mind let us consult, as an example, the proposal for a Council framework decision on the principle of availability.[31] In the very first paragraph of the explanatory memorandum the Commission suggests that the objective of developing an 'Area of Freedom, Security and Justice' requires 'a new principle for the exchange of law enforcement information, which entails that information needed for the fight against crime should cross the internal borders of the EU without obstacles'.[32] In order to account for why there is a justification for drawing such an overt link between the development of the AFSJ and the technical issue of the exchange of data between Member States, the Commission states: 'the central role of information exchange in the security gambit of the Union became apparent after the abolition of controls at the internal borders pursuant to the Schengen Convention'.[33] Hence the issue of borders and free movement of persons is strongly associated with the issue of security but, in addition, once the 'security' problem has been identified then the way is open for this to be resolved, or managed, by developing systems of better and more efficient data exchange. A further example of this way of thinking can be given if we consider the proposal for a Council decision concerning access for consultation of the Visa Information

29 Ibid., para. 2.

30 Ibid., para. 4. At para. 13 there is a further example: 'One of the objectives of this plan is to propose mechanisms for working and co-operating at the European Union level which will permit those responsible for checks and surveillance at the external borders of the European Union to co-ordinate their operational actions and to arrive at a coherent framework for common action in the medium to long term'.

31 COM (2005) 490.

32 Ibid., p. 2.

33 Ibid., p. 2.

System (VIS).[34] Once again the opening paragraph presupposes the fundamental link between advanced information systems and security and, in particular, the continued progress of the AFSJ as a form of management of security risks:

> These [measures] aim at increasing co-operation in fields ranging from intelligence sharing to law enforcement in order to make it easier to find, detain and bring to justice terror suspects, in promoting and ensuring security while preserving and reinforcing individual rights and freedoms.[35]

There seems to be ample support for the conclusion that the rationale behind many of the measures taking place is a strong understanding that free movement of persons, within the borders of the EU, requires a relationship with practices of security. In effect the borders of the EU become significant to our political lives only in so far as they can be rendered secure. As we have already noted, the security of free movement across the borders of the EU takes a number of different forms but there is a prominent trend towards technological modes of surveillance and information exchange, which are also described as 'soft security'. The crucial matter that arises, however, is the extent to which such practices can be meaningful in constituting an *area* of freedom, security and justice. This issue is the focal point of the chapter and concerns the extent to which such practices, which relate the issue of space to security, can support the necessary common commitment to freedom, security and justice as manifested in the *area* of freedom, security and justice. What is at stake is how we can sustain an understanding of the AFSJ as representing constitutional public goods and therefore respond to concerns about the constitutional legitimacy provoked by the AFSJ integration.

What are the Constitutional Implications?

What do these legal practices about security and freedom of movement reveal about our constitutional commitments? This is a question which brings together the more general reflections about constitutional legitimacy, in earlier chapters, and ties them to an interpretation of the concrete practices of the AFSJ. We have already concluded that what is taking place in the AFSJ raises questions of constitutional concern, but now the task is a different one: do the practices of the AFSJ enable us to relate our constitutional concerns about the AFSJ to the wider issue of the commitments to a constitutional way of life, or are we faced with a serious dilemma whereby the current way that integration is proceeding in the AFSJ obscures and prevents us from understanding it in constitutional terms?

A number of different strands of thought have already been developed and the task now is to bring them together and so provide some conclusions about

34 See Commission Document, COM (2005) 600.

35 Ibid., p. 3.

the prospects for thinking about constitutional legitimacy for the AFSJ, and the difficulties that we face in this respect. The first strand relates to what has already been established, in the previous chapter, about the nature of security as a constitutional public good. Security has become increasingly associated with the technologies of governing a population (governmentality) and this, it was claimed, has led to difficulties in being able to understand security as a constitutional public good (as the basis for political trust and common commitments). The second strand is that the representation of area or space is one that necessarily presupposes a common constitutional commitment (a common political way of life as relating to space) and that there are grave dangers about pursuing the representation of legal space without this constitutive feature. Finally, the third strand, recently considered, is the relationship between free movement of persons within the borders of the EU (and the consequent positing of external borders) and the increasing tendency for this to be achieved in conjunction with security practices, in particular, the technological techniques of surveillance and information sharing.

A recent contribution by the scholar of International Relations and Security Studies, Didier Bigo, provides an appropriate point of departure for a consideration of the wider constitutional meanings latent in current practices. Regarding free movement, security and operational techniques, Bigo writes:

> The notion of freedom is reconfigured to develop control and surveillance of people at the external borders and through visas in their own country … the influence of a neo-conservative agenda, that reframes liberty by distorting the concept in the name of the defence of an 'essentialized' *us* under threat by unknown *others* …[36]

And then later on:

> The terms freedom and justice exist then in the Hague Programme but their meanings are reconfigured as lower values in the name of the priority of security and, ultimately, the concept of freedom is profoundly changed.[37]

These two passages convey a number of features that require further attention. Bigo uses the idea of 'reconfiguration' to suggest that the values of freedom and justice are pursued, or developed, in such a way that they form part of security; they are reconfigured as part of the 'security agenda'. Here it becomes important to consider what this implies. It is worth noting that, in so far as security is a public good, it would be a mistake to interpret matters in this way: namely that there

---

36 See Didier Bigo 'Liberty, Whose Liberty? The Hague Programme and the Conception of Freedom' in *Security Versus Freedom: A Challenge for Europe's Future*, edited by Thierry Balzacq and Sergio Carrera (Aldershot: Ashgate, 2006) at p. 37; the emphasis is the author's own.

37 Ibid., p. 41.

are the goods of freedom and justice on one side of the scale, and security on the other, or that security is necessarily detrimental to, or the antithesis of, political trust.[38] Instead, Bigo seems to argue that freedom and justice measures *are* security measures. Taken on its own such a claim would not make sense because how are we to decide which factual information forms part of 'freedom' and which 'security', unless we are to have an *a priori* definition of security and freedom. However, what we are told by Bigo is that in practice 'freedom is reconfigured to develop control and surveillance systems …' Here, then, we arrive at the critical issue. What Bigo seems to suggest is that it is only possible to make sense of the current practices if *both* freedom and security have become reduced to issues of control and surveillance; this becomes the 'predominance of security'.

In reality the 'predominance of security' refers to the predominance of technologies of security which distorts both our sense of freedom *and* security. The current practice of free movement aligned to the technologies of security conceals how security must be part of our understanding of our common commitments to an *area* of freedom, security and justice. It is security, in this more constitutional sense, which is potentially at risk in the current practices. In the following analysis I would like to explore more fully, and by engagement with the legal practices, the implications for how this instrumental view of security might distort constitutional life.

One of the most apparent components of a technology of security can be identified as a control over a population;[39] in fact the term population itself arises as data that is gathered concerning a people. It has already been noted how there has arisen a trend, concerning the development of security strategies, which advocates a targeting of population through profiling or the monitoring of 'sub-groups'.[40] Hence, technology refines and focuses the control that can be attained concerning the individuals within a group or population. As Levi and Wall remark it is the possibility, which enhanced technology allows, of focusing on the individual or sub-groups within the population that corresponds to the 'panopticon' paradigm of surveillance.[41] The extent to which the practices of surveillance become ever

38 Although Bigo does not advocate such a view of security; he does, however, commit himself to the idea that freedom and security are conceptually different. So for instance, on p. 38, he claims that 'Freedom, security and the relation between the two concepts can be analysed along different lines of thought. So, the idea of a straightforward balance between liberty and security is distorted by the fact that some conceptualizations do not recognize the autonomy of the two scales'. Whilst this is an understandable conclusion it is highly rationalistic and unfortunately does no justice to the extent to which security must be said to be relationship of meaning with other public goods, as I argued at length previously to this chapter.

39 For further discussion, see previous chapter.

40 See, Michael Levi and David Wall, 'Technologies, Security and Privacy in the Post 9/11 European Information Society', p. 200.

41 The 'panopticon' of surveillance become an architectural feature of the organisation of space in order to make the surveillance of prisoners permanent and to ensure

more 'focused' on the individual can be seen in relation to those measures that act on the body by gathering and manipulating biological data also referred to as 'biometric data'. A number of measures relating to free movement make use of advances in technology which allow security measures to be exercised against the body: for instance, passports contain iris recognition schemes,[42] and notably the *Eurodac* database which holds the fingerprint data of adult asylum seekers. *Eurodac* supports efforts of Member States towards establishing an asylum policy and implementation of the Dublin Convention,[43] an instrument whereby the responsibility for asylum, and the care of the seeker of asylum, is to be shared amongst the Member States.[44] The creation of such a Europe-wide system of co-operation regarding where an asylum seeker ought to be and which Member State should be processing the application demanded a system capable of processing this sort of data. *Eurodac*[45] was established for the purposes of creating, and storing, a database of fingerprints and accompanying personal data so as to ensure that each individual asylum seeker could be identified across the common scheme of asylum in the EU.

Elspeth Guild acknowledges that the *Eurodac* system seeks to locate, and categorise, the *body* of the asylum seeker, and so supports the reading of the technologies of security as a power which acts on the body of a population, or bio-power.[46] Guild helpfully clarifies some of the practical implications that can emerge from this by providing a specific example. In 2005 a case came before the High Court concerning a Sudanese man who was applying for asylum in the United Kingdom.[47] When he had applied for asylum in the UK, the authorities had carried out a check on him using the common EU database, and found out that he had first applied for asylum in Italy. He was therefore transferred back to Italy in order to complete the asylum process. It transpired that Mr Ali had not first been registered in Italy; there had been some mistake and when the Italian authorities took his fingerprints and compared them against the database they found that he was not the same person as the individual first registered in Italy. Therefore, he was not able to make an asylum application in Italy and consequently was not entitled to the care, shelter and food that the Italian Government would have had to provide him had his identity been legitimate. No action was taken to rectify

the permanent presence of power. See Michel Foucault, *Discipline and Punish: The Birth of the Prison* (London: Penguin Books, 1991) in particular, see Chapter 3, 'panopticonism'.

42 Council Regulation EC 2252/2004, 'Standards for Security Features and biometrics in passports and travel documents', OJ L 385/1.

43 Now amended by Council Regulation No 343/2003; OJ L 50/1.

44 That is to say in order to discharge the responsibilities for the asylum seeker that are contained in the Geneva Convention.

45 Established under Council Regulation 2725/2000; OJ L 316.

46 See the reference to the work of Foucault in the previous chapter.

47 The case, as Elspeth Guild mentions, goes unreported because the British government conceded liability: *The Queen on the application of Mr Numieri Mohammed Ali v Secretary of State for the Home Department* CO/1472/2005.

the error, and, as Mr Ali had no family or resources he had to rely on charity for assistance and aid.[48] After formal applications were made to the British Courts the authorities in the UK recognised the error and Mr Ali was sent back to the UK.

It is quite right, as an initial reaction, to suggest that a situation as unfortunate as this, and as personally difficult for Mr Ali, is bound to occur in any system. We know and appreciate, as a matter of pragmatism if nothing else, that mistakes and errors are probable and do happen, no matter how hard we might try to ensure a perfect system. However, the technical fallibility of a system like *Eurodac* is not actually the issue that concerns Elspeth Guild here:

> The body of the asylum seeker becomes the traceable evidence of his or her existence. The existence in law of the asylum seeker as a person seeking a right to reside, access to the labour markets or benefits remain allocated to a Member State ... In the EURODAC system the body of the asylum seeker becomes increasingly separated from an essential element of his or her legal personality; the right to be present. The body takes on an identity and is followed via its fingerprint data across borders while that of the body's legal personality which gives the right to be present remains trapped in one jurisdiction.[49]

At one level what Elspeth Guild writes could be taken as a pragmatic suggestion – that more needs to be done at the EU level to ensure that there is a greater emphasis placed upon the needs and care of asylum seekers such that there can be efficient help, support and resources for someone who might find themselves in the sort of situation that Mr Ali found himself in. This may well be sensible, and depending on issues of financial resources such considerations might eventually receive due attention at the EU level. There is, however, a further reading that I would like to offer, one that poses a more challenging consideration of matters relating to the technology of security and the impact this has on the notion of being inside an area of commitment to constitutional public goods. What is of concern is the extent to which the process of information gathering and exchange can lead to an increasing dislocation as to the location of the common political experience. Technological developments enable an increasingly abstract experience of constitutionalism to take place which may not necessarily be grounded in 'being present' or 'being involved' in any location, and this leads to a dislocation between the individual and place. This is a difficult and rather abstract idea, but it is very much related to the discussion of 'engagement in practices' in constitutional public goods and also the legal construction of area – for if we are to experience a concerned engagement with the constitutional practices then we must acknowledge that there is a connection between the package of legal responsibilities and rights and

48 The Italian Refugee Council.

49 Elspeth Guild, 'The Bitter Fruits of a Common Asylum Policy', in *Security Versus Freedom: A Challenge for Europe's Future*, edited by Thierry Balzacq and Sergio Carrera, pp. 61–76.

the 'body' or the physical location in which we experience this legal personality. The difficulty is that, to a certain extent, the technical management of our legal personality, as a matter of security, may always tend towards impersonality. Hence it is abstracted from our sense of proximity to, and experience of, constitutional life and therefore the task is to recognise and think about this.

What has Been the Response?

How have the EU institutions approached concerns over the tendency to understand security with technological sharing, surveillance and operational efficiency, in the process of developing the right to free movement in the EU? Above all, what can we learn about how we understand the deep constitutional concerns that arise when how we relate to legal space in the EU becomes distorted by the technologies of security?

In considering the practices of security and the connection with free movement several references were made to the documents released by the EU institutions. As well as explaining the general reasons behind the need for, say, the Schengen Information System or the Visa Information System, these documents also provide some clues as to the constitutional issues posed by such measures, and as such are important documents to consider. The Commission, as policy developers, are aware that many of the surveillance and operational activities they propose do raise questions that are constitutional; this is perceived mainly through the prism as to how such practices affect the political rights of individuals. Consequently, there are claims that the security scheme proposed contains measures which will safeguard human rights and ensure that sensitive data about people, which is gathered and stored, is properly protected. As an example, consider this statement in the Proposal for a Council Decision on the establishment, operation and use of the second generation Schengen Information System (SIS II):

> In order to ensure consistent and homogenous application of the data protection rules regarding SIS II, the Decision provides for the application of Regulation EC 45/2001 on the protection of individuals with regard to the processing of personal data and entrusts the European Data Protection Supervisor with the monitoring of the personal data processing activities related to the SIS II carried out by the Commission in accordance with the Decision.[50]

This statement reveals how the Commission proposes to resolve the problem of how to protect individuals from any possible data abuse. The measure is to follow a document, called the Data Protection Directive, which sets down guidelines concerning the appropriate means and purposes of processing personal data; and further that this process will be monitored by an expert official, 'European Data

50 See COM (2005) 230; OJ L 2007/205 at p. 3.

Supervisor'.[51] It is certain that this may be seen as a sufficient and adequate mode of protection: provided oversight and procedural restrictions are followed, protection of peoples' data, and therefore their freedom, is ensured. However, we must allow the inquiry to go much deeper and ask what does such a scheme presuppose about the constitutional issues, and how they can be resolved?

Given that this is the task let us consider a further example, from the Council Framework Decision on the exchange of information under the principle of availability. In this passage the author(s) of the document reveal how a concern to protect fundamental rights becomes important in drafting the proposed framework decision:

> The Commission organised two rounds of consultations with stakeholders in the area of exchange of data for the purpose of making possible, facilitate or accelerate the prevention, detection or investigation of criminal offences. The consultations explored the concept of the principle of availability, and gave feedback on implementation strategies and on more effective ways to protect fundamental rights.[52]

The document provides details as to the stakeholders and, in general terms, what they advised:

> On the 23rd November 2004 and 8th March 2005 consultations were organised with representatives of human rights interest groups and the Committee of the European Parliament, to receive feedback on the concerns of civil society … the consultation with representatives of human rights interest groups and of the European Parliament focussed mainly on the traceability of each step in the information exchange chain to underpin meaningful legal remedies.[53]

This advice finds its way into a special clause in the proposed framework decision where one of the general grounds to refuse a request for information is to 'protect the fundamental rights and freedoms of persons whose data is processed'.[54] Such a clause indicates that the advice of the 'human rights stakeholders' was considered and then drafted into the legislation in order that there might be an adequate restraint and accountability system in place against possible abuses of the system.

I would like to argue that these two examples, taken from two policy documents which concern the security dimension of the issue of freedom of movement, reveal some underlying presuppositions about the institutional response to the constitutional issues raised by these sorts of policy proposals. In each case there

51 The current supervisor is Peter Hustinx and further information as to his role can be found on the website at: http://www.edps.europa.eu/EDPSWEB/edps/lang/en/pid/1.

52 COM (2005) 490 at p. 5.

53 Ibid.

54 Ibid., Article 14(d), p. 20.

is a reference to an external sort of expertise; in one, it is the independent office of a 'Data Protection Supervisor'; in the other, 'stakeholders'.[55] Each either supervises the operation of the measure or provides advice in the construction of the proposal. Also a set of abstract rights and duties are referred to either in the form of 'data protections rights and laws'[56] or 'fundamental rights and freedoms'. A certain faith, therefore, is placed in the ability of abstract rules, procedures and a body of experts to restrain and to provide an oversight of the practices of surveillance, information gathering work and operational efficiency of security measures.

There are those who more or less endorse this approach to confronting the constitutional questions raised by these security practices. Evelien Brouwer writes:

> The legal framework of the EU data surveillance architecture will be highly important, not only for the protection of individual rights, but also for the possibility of independent authorities to scrutinize the use of these systems … currently the powers and means of independent data authorities are limited. Future legislation should at least include the possibility to impose heavy fines on governments which act in breach of the applicable rules and supervisory authorities should be equipped with sufficient means and staff to fulfil their tasks.[57]

Accordingly she advises that the supervisory rules and procedures be strengthened by imposing fines for egregious breaches of data rights or fundamental freedoms and adequate resources be given to expert overseers. The importance of human rights accountability is also discussed by Steve Peers. For instance, with regard to the issue of data protection he remarks: 'it should be also kept in mind that the right to respect for private life, set out in Article 8 [of the European Convention on Human Rights], also comprises a right to the protection of personal data, which is increasingly relevant in the areas of visas and border controls'.[58]

A continuation of this rationale can also be found in the most recent programmatic measures for the AFSJ in the Stockholm agenda (2009) in which the Council, in setting out the terms of reference for the Commission, offers a robust view of the 'management of information':

---

55 As point of interest about the use of language; holding a stake or having a stake derives its meaning from something which is placed in hazard, which is to be guaranteed by winning a game or competition. More specifically this is associated with gambling or placing a wager but can also be used in the business sense of 'having a stake in the company' where one's investment is what is gambled, or wagered, or 'at stake'.

56 The Data Protection Directive, 95/46/EC.

57 See Evelien Brouwer, 'Data Surveillance and Border Control in the EU', in *Security Versus Freedom: A Challenge for Europe's Future*, at p. 153.

58 Steve Peers, *Justice and Home Affairs*, p. 121.

> implement[ing] an EU Information Strategy, which includes a strong data protection regime. Development must be coherent with the priorities set out for the area of freedom, security and justice and the internal security strategy, supporting the vision for law enforcement, judicial co-operation, border management and public protection.[59]

Conclusion

The foregoing discussion has revealed features of the practices that constitute the relationship between free movement and security in the AFSJ. This relationship has been characterised by a tendency towards surveillance techniques, technological oversight and operational efficiency, displaying those elements of a technology of security that we encountered in the previous chapter. The representation of the *area* of freedom, security and justice becomes inextricably bound up with the concerns over security and, in particular, the need to control the migrant population of EU citizens and non-citizens. As was mentioned at the outset it is clear that the representation that the EU as an *area* is commitment to the realisation of certain public goods (freedom, security and justice) implies or presupposes a sense of 'common interest'. Indeed, in attempting to understand the EU's response to concerns that the practices of security technology undermine the constitutional legitimacy of integration in the AFSJ the Commission, as we have considered, has attempted to bolster the protection through a range of legal procedures for citizens and non-citizens concerning fundamental rights and data protections. It can be seen that such a response is an attempt to understand the constitutional implications and to acknowledge the concerns about the practices of security technology.

The question to pose, and consider, is what mode of understanding constitutionalism is bound up with this response. The Commission documents revealed a strong commitment to a form of constitutional response that can be recognised as based on restraint. There is a confidence that legal rules and procedures will provide a 'check and balance' on the operation of the security measures. The response seems to fall into the conventional understanding of constitutional legitimacy which we explored in Chapter 2. If we recall, in summary, what was considered there, the most conventional form of constitutional legitimacy (by this I mean an understanding which is the presupposition of most constitutional arrangements) is that the legitimate authority of political life is established by placing legally defined limits on the scope of the political agency. Whilst there can be no doubt that this is an adequate description of the purpose of most Constitutions it does not resolve the legitimacy problem of constitutional life. Constitutional legitimacy, therefore, did not derive from the legally constituted constitution but the involvement or participation in a tradition of common

---

59 The Council of the European Union, 'The Stockholm Programme – An Open and Secure Europe Serving and Protecting the Citizens'. Para. 4.2.2 Doc. 17024/09.

constitutional commitment. In respect of the constitutional legitimacy of the AFSJ I interpreted this as being a common commitment to freedom, security and justice as constitutional public goods. In other words, the legal rules and procedures cannot alone supply the legitimacy of constitutional life. To what extent does the institutional response of the EU acknowledge this dimension in respect of the constitutional concerns of free movement and security? Clearly the institutional response assumes that increased procedural fairness and a clear structure of fundamental rights and data protection will provide a constitutional legitimacy in respect of the practices of technological security that we have considered so far. There is some room to be sceptical as to whether the sorts of measures based in the restraint view of constitutionalism will be able to achieve this. The difficulty can be illustrated if we return to the central dilemma as to how we understand membership of a political community; we have already seen that many of the practices of positing the borders of the EU call into question the way in which we are able to understand ourselves as political agents such that we can participate in the commitments to an *area* of freedom, security and justice. It is a concern not so much about the rights we have as citizens to call into question the worst excesses of surveillance abuse but the gradual shift that these practices effect in the way that we can understand the possibilities of political involvement. For instance, consider how Juliet Lodge describes what she dubs the 'proximity paradox' in respect of information technologies:

> At the very time when technology has made it possible to bring the EU closer to the citizen more directly than ever before, EU citizens and residents appear to be more suspicious of it than ever before. The proximity paradox resides therefore in the tension between their sense of closeness and the semblance of closeness that ICTs offer everyone within the EU's common border. ICTs create the illusion of transparency and openness without the substance of open, democratically visible and credible political accountability and control.[60]

This is a succinct observation, which draws attention to the closing of ways of understanding political participation by the over emphasis on certain modes of information technologies. Similar concerns can be found in Theodora Kostakopolou's account of the need to reconfigure citizenship in the EU as 'constructive':

> The main task of citizenship theory is to articulate a narrative which takes into account these developments and the complexity of our era, without retreating into a nostalgia for a 'politics of place' or to the romanticism of 'embeddedness' in organic communities. As an alternative conception of community which

60 Juliet Lodge, 'Transparency, Justice and Territoriality: The EU Border Challenge', in *Security Versus Freedom*, at p. 275. ICTs refer to Information and Communication Technologies.

> respects the Other, *I suggest the notion of community of concern and engagement. In such a community, all its corporate and individual members – associated by virtue of their difference from one another – share a common concern over the nature and the future of the polity and are engaged in collectively shaping that future*'.[61]

It is such an understanding of political membership that is neglected by the current practices of the AFSJ which have become strongly attached to a security agenda which sees modes of surveillance and biometric data as central to delivering the secure free movement of people in the EU.

The way in which a political and legal community relates to space through common commitments and the shared participation in their meaning becomes a central facet of constitutional life. However, it is precisely this relational understanding of space that can become neglected in circumstances in which the act of closing the legal space becomes one of control and management. The *area* of freedom, security and justice exhibits precisely this tendency to neglect the need to relate to space in favour of a series of legal practices in which the technologies of security are accorded prominence. It is not easy to ensure that we acknowledge constitutional life in circumstances where there is a strong practical need to guarantee the security of the borders of the EU; and yet it is also very difficult to assess the consequences and implications of what we are neglecting by such practices. This chapter has offered an interpretation of what our current practices may mean in so far as we address ourselves to concerns over the constitutional legitimacy of these practices. Nevertheless, the questions about how to direct, or alter, the current practices do not really lie within the domain of conceptual or theoretical reflection; instead, and as I stressed in the introduction to the chapter, they lie within our practical involvement or concern with those practices.

61 Theodora Kostakopoulou, *Citizenship, Identity and Immigration in the European Union: Between Past and Future* (Manchester: Manchester University Press, 2001) at p. 103.

Chapter 6
Constitutional Life and Criminal Justice

Introduction

The practices of criminal justice provide the possibility of a further insight into the constitutional difficulties confronting the AFSJ. Criminal justice poses the connection between the constitutional commitments to the public goods of freedom, security and justice and the representation of a legally constituted *area* (the positing of borders and the regulation of the movement of persons across borders by criminal sanction). In other words, it might be thought that the connection between criminal legal practices and constitutional life is readily ascertainable or discernable. Perhaps the clearest reason for this lies in the connection between criminal law and political authority. It is almost axiomatic that the criminal legal sanction both represents and actively reinforces the sovereign authority of the state; all criminal prosecutions are carried out in the name of the state and the sanction or punishment imposed upon the individual carries with it important symbolic indication concerning the relationship between the individual and membership of the state.[1] Precisely because criminal justice has become so intertwined with the claim to sovereign authority (of the state) it poses considerable difficulties for the AFSJ where criminal justice measures are developed without the same claim to legitimate constitutional (or sovereign) authority. Criminal justice measures, therefore, lie at the very centre of the constitutional questions facing the AFSJ (and therefore the EU) and reinforce the need to reflect constitutionally upon the legitimacy of these developments. This chapter examines the depth of the connection between criminal justice and issues of constitutional legitimacy in order to consider both the acknowledgement of the AFSJ of this constitutional dimension and, as in the previous chapter, an evaluation of the practices.

---

1 See, for example the discussion by Kimmo Nuotio on the criminal law and its relationship with constitutional symbolism: 'On the Significance of Criminal Justice for a Europe "United in Diversity"', in *Europe in Search of Meaning and Purpose*, edited by Kimmo Nuotio (Helsinki: University of Helsinki Publications, 2004).

Criminal Law and the Common Area of Justice

There exists a significant, and growing, corpus of substantive criminal law stemming from the third pillar competence in the field of co-operation on criminal justice.[2] There are now common EU offences for:

- counterfeiting currency;[3]
- counterfeiting non-cash instruments;[4]
- money-laundering;[5]
- terrorism;[6]
- trafficking in persons;[7]
- drug trafficking;[8]
- child prostitution and pornography offences;[9]
- racism and xenophobia;[10]
- organised crime;[11]
- attacks on information systems;[12] and
- environmental crime.[13]

---

2 Although, as remarked upon early in Chapter 3, this has been slightly complicated by the fact that the ECJ has been rather keen to imply an EC competence to enact criminal law in the area of environmental legislation, see Case C-176/03 *Commission of the European Communities v Council of the European Union.*

3 With the introduction of the Euro there needed to be specific European-wide measures; see Council Framework Decision, 2002/888/JHA [2001] OJ L 329/3.

4 Council Framework Decision, 2001/413/JHA, combating fraud and counterfeiting of non-cash means of payment [2001] OJ L 149/1.

5 Council Framework Decision, 2001/500/JHA 'on money laundering, the identification, tracing, freezing, seizing and confiscation of instrumentalities and the proceeds of crime' [2001] OJ L 182/1.

6 Council Framework Decision, 2002/475/JHA 'on combating terrorism' [2002] OJ L 164/3.

7 Council Framework Decision, 2002/629/JHA 'on combating trafficking in human beings' [2002] OJ L 203/1.

8 Council Framework Decision, 2004/757/JHA 'laying down minimum provisions on the constituent elements of criminal acts and penalties in the field of illicit drug trafficking' [2004] OJ L 335/8.

9 Council Framework Decision, 2004/68/JHA 'on combating the sexual exploitation of children and child pornography' [2004] OJ L 13/44.

10 Framework Decision 2008/913/JHA on combating certain forms and expressions of racism and xenophobia by means of criminal law [2008] OJ L 328/55.

11 Framework Decision 2008/841/JHA on the fight against organised crime [2008] OJ L 300/42.

12 Framework Decision 2005/222/JHA on attacks against information systems [2005] OJ L69/67.

13 Framework Decision 2005/667/JHA to strengthen the criminal law framework for the enforcement of the law against ship-source pollution [2005] OJ L 225/164.

These measures have been developed through the third pillar instrument, the framework decision, (Article 34 TEU) and therefore through the inter-governmental legislative procedures of the third pillar, which I outlined in the Chapter 1. The Treaty on the Functioning of the European Union (TFEU) which came into force at the end of 2009 promises to significantly alter the way in which criminal law legislation can be developed in the EU. Co-operation in criminal justice will now be subject to the co-decision procedure or the 'ordinary legislative procedure' of the former Community pillar; in addition, it will be possible for the Court of Justice to gain full powers of judicial review in respect of the interpretation of criminal justice measures.[14] Finally, the TFEU also provides, under Article 86, the legal basis for the establishment of the Office of European Public Prosecutor for the investigation and prosecution of financial crimes against the EU and also those crimes with a serious cross-border component.

The augmentation of the powers of the EU, in the old-third pillar matters, is reflected in a more ambitious set of measures in the Stockholm Programme (2009). In the Council's communication to the Commission, in advance of the drawing up of the Action Plan, the importance of criminal law harmonisation is highlighted:

> In the face of cross-border crime, more efforts should be made to make judicial cooperation more efficient ... for example the approximation, where necessary, of substantive and procedural law should facilitate mutual recognition.[15]

Further, in Article 83(1) TFEU, provision is made concerning the basis upon which full harmonisation of criminal law (provision of common definition and sanction) is to proceed where the crime is particularly serious with a cross-border dimension and needs to be combated on a common basis.

It must also not be forgotten that in addition to the issue concerning the harmonisation of substantive provisions of criminal law there is also a significant body of common procedural law; the most notable example of this is the framework decision on the European Arrest Warrant (EAW) which has transformed how extraditions take place between Member States in the EU. More recently there have been a plethora of procedural measures intended to aid the co-operation between justice officials in Member States over aspects of evidence exchange[16] and enhancing the procedural rights of suspects.[17] Many of the measures undertaken by the EU on criminal matters state their aim as enhancing 'mutual recognition' as

14 Article 263 TFEU.

15 Council Communication 'The Stockholm Programme', para. 3.1.

16 Council Framework Decision 2008/978/JHA on the European evidence warrant for the purpose of obtaining objects, documents and data for use in proceedings in criminal matters [2008] OJ L 350.

17 Council Framework Decision 2009/299/JHA of 26 February 2009 amending Framework Decisions 2002/584/JHA, 2005/214/JHA, 2008/909/JHA and 2008/947/JHA, thereby enhancing the procedural rights of persons and fostering the application of the

opposed to a harmonisation of criminal law across the Member States. It becomes important to distinguish between these two doctrines of legal integration and to understand the extent to which they bear upon the question as to whether there exists something like a common area of criminal justice across the EU.

In discussing the 'transformation' of criminal law in the AFSJ Mitsilegas notes the importance played by ideas of effectiveness and application of law derived from the Community or common market legal experience.[18] This is not completely surprising, although, as will be developed in more depth, it does raise serious questions concerning the distinction between economic and criminal integration. Even in the context of the internal market there has been a shift away from the view that legal integration entails the creation of 'total harmonization' of legal measures across Member States. Michael Dougan remarks that one of the most prominent reasons for this is the expansion of policy away from common market values and principles of ensuring the most expeditious legal regime for the free movement of goods, persons, services and capital across borders and towards a wider (and potentially opposing) set of values: *inter alia* environmental protection; consumer rights; social policy; education and training; culture; public health; law and order. The effect has been to ensure that integration and harmonization now becomes implicated in the way values are balanced at the EU level:

> These factors also throw light on the rising tide of differentiation within the Community legal order. Traditional regulatory techniques such as total harmonization have not single-mindedly been maintained because it became necessary *to balance the Community's original objectives of maintaining a genuinely level playing field ... against the desire for Member States to have differing levels of social provision.*[19]

European level integration must recognise the differing national attitudes concerning policy on non-economic matters and therefore allow and enable a certain flexibility of regulatory diversity. Dougan envisages, however, that such a situation will require a negotiation between European and national levels concerning the appropriate mode of ensuring that a common and co-operative functioning of the internal market is able to proceed, notwithstanding variations in regulatory frameworks. Here he sees an important role for lawyers and in particular courts:

---

principle of mutual recognition to decisions rendered in the absence of the person concerned at the trial [2009] OJ L 81.

18 Valsamis Mitsilegas, 'The Transformation of Criminal Law in the Area of Freedom, Security and Justice', 26 *Yearbook of European Law* (2007), pp. 1–32.

19 Michael Dougan, 'Minimum Harmonization and the Internal Market', 37 *Common Market Law Review* (2000), pp. 853–885 at p. 862. My emphasis.

> It is equally possible that in a dispute over the validity of additional national regulation which turns ultimately on the correct legal basis of the relevant community secondary legislation, the Court may be faced with a choice between advancing the internal market by encouraging uniformity, and protecting vulnerable social interests by permitting regulatory diversity.[20]

It is this shift in emphasis – whereby legal integration is enhanced and developed through the channels of co-operation between the courts of Member States and the European Union – that becomes most apparent in the context of establishing a common area of criminal justice. It was recognised, from early on, that there would only be sufficient consensus on relatively few areas of criminal law for the Member States to pursue total harmonisation. However, even if harmonisation of criminal law only occurred in those few instances where there was a common European-wide interest in establishing a minimum legal regime on a particular matter there needed to be some way of promoting enhanced levels of co-operation and trust in the common area of criminal justice. To this extent it was decided, at the European Council meeting at Cardiff in 1998, to investigate the possibility of using the principle of mutual recognition, derived from common market principles, in the enforcement of decisions and judgments in criminal matters.

The Commission was involved in the development of the principle of mutual recognition in terms of substantive proposals and measures, under the general remit provided by the Treaty of Amsterdam (1997), which formed the basis of the Action Plans of Tampere and Hague. It therefore becomes necessary to explore how the Commission advances, and indeed understands, the term 'the principle of mutual recognition'; and to this end the document entitled *Communication from the Commission to the Council and the European Parliament: Mutual Recognition of Final Decisions in Criminal Matters*[21] reveals something of the underlying presuppositions concerning mutual recognition. To begin with there is an outline as to how the traditional or conventional means of obtaining co-operation in criminal matters works:

> Traditional judicial co-operation in criminal matters is based on a variety of international legal instruments, which are overwhelmingly characterised by what one might call the request principle: one sovereign state makes a request to another sovereign state, who then determines whether it will or will not comply with the request. Sometimes, the rules on compliance are rather strict, not leaving much of a choice; on other occasions, the requesting state must await the reply to its request before it gets what its authorities need in order to pursue a criminal case.[22]

---

20 Michael Dougan, 'Minimum Harmonization and the Internal Market', p. 882.

21 COM (2000) 495 (final).

22 Ibid., p. 2.

This process was found to be slow, cumbersome and fairly unpredictable and so the principle of mutual recognition serves to improve this situation by, in the Commission's view:

> borrowing from concepts that have worked very well in the creation of the Single Market, the idea was born that juridical co-operation might also benefit from the concept of mutual recognition, which simply stated, means that once a certain measure, such as a decision taken by a judge in exercising his or her official powers in one member state, has been taken, that measure – in so far as it has external implications – would automatically be accepted in all other Member States, and have the same or at least similar effects there.[23]

It is a straightforward idea that a decision, or judgment, in one Member State is accepted by another even if that decision or judgment would not have been decided in the same (or similar) way. What underlies such an idea? Although it may seem to be a simple solution to encourage judicial co-operation, it is possible to appreciate that it will not be particularly easy, in practice, to require courts to accept that a decision or judgment taken in another criminal jurisdiction must be accorded recognition and enforcement, even though there may be very many substantive practical differences between the two systems. The Commission attempts to respond to this by suggesting that the idea of mutual recognition is governed by an abstract principle of 'trust'. Consider the following passage:

> Mutual trust is an important element, not only trust in the adequacy of one's partners' rules, but also that these rules are correctly applied. Based on this idea of equivalence and the trust it is based on, the results the state has reached are allowed to take into effect in one's own sphere of legal influence.[24]

The principle of mutual recognition in criminal matters is now enshrined in Article 82 TFEU, stating that: 'judicial co-operation in criminal matters in the Union shall be based on the principle of mutual recognition of judgments and judicial decisions...'. Here are values of trust and mutual recognition that seem to encapsulate how the different criminal justice systems can work in partnership, whilst avoiding the need for direct measures which aim at full or even partial harmonisation of entire tracts of substantive criminal law or procedure.

I would like to come back directly to consider the issue of 'trust' at a later juncture, as this connects the issue of criminal justice measures with constitutionalism. However, for the time being I would like to consider how the issue of a common area of criminal justice has been advanced through the principle of *ne bis in idem* and how this augments our understanding of the importance of mutual recognition.

---

23 Ibid.

24 Ibid., p. 4.

The creation of a common European criminal justice system, founded on trust and the practice of mutual recognition, is highlighted in the development of the principle of *ne bis in idem* by the European Court of the Justice. Commonly known as the double jeopardy rule this is the legal principle that a person cannot face multiple prosecutions for the same offence. In the transnational context *ne bis in idem* becomes translated into the idea that a person cannot be prosecuted twice, in the different jurisdictions, for a transnational offence involving more than one jurisdiction; in practice this means that one of the interested state parties seeking prosecution will have to relinquish this in favour of another Member State. A number of significant ambiguities about how such a principle could operate in the European context led to an important preliminary reference to the European Court of Justice. In *Gözütok and Brügge*[25] (conjoined) the appellants were subject to prosecution in one Member State, which was discontinued by the prosecuting authorities once the defendant paid a certain sum of money. This decision to discontinue was purely administrative; in other words, there was no court or tribunal involved in the process. It then occurred that another Member State asserted a cause in the proceedings and issued a further prosecution of the same person on the basis of the same facts. It was held by the ECJ that this was not permissible, as the *ne bis in idem* rule also covered these sorts of 'administrative' prosecution procedures.[26]

The result or state of affairs to be avoided is one where an individual faces multiple criminal prosecutions on the same facts in different Member States simply for availing him or herself of the right to freely move across the internal borders. So much is plain, as the Advocate General in the case remarks: Article 54,[27] 'is the expression of that safeguard for persons who are subject to the exercise of the *ius puniendi*'.[28] However, the rule is not to be seen as simply a procedural safeguard for the individual because a consideration as to how the individual is to be protected, in such circumstances, becomes a matter of deeper constitutional significance concerning the common meanings and values shared in a European context which is asserting the existence of a common area of justice. In this respect consider the following passage from the Advocate General's opinion:

---

25 Cases C-187/01 and C385/01; [2003] ECR I-1345. The case was based upon an interpretation of Article 54 of the Convention Implementing the Schengen Convention; it is seen as providing a commitment to the principle of *ne bis in idem* in the EU which states: 'A person whose trial has been finally disposed of in one Contracting Party may not be prosecuted in another contracting party for the same acts provided that, if a penalty has been imposed, it has been enforced under the laws of the sentencing Contracting Party'.

26 In particular, see para. 48 of the judgment.

27 See above for details of the legal text.

28 Opinion of Advocate General Ruiz-Jarabo Colomer, delivered 19 September 2002, see para. 46.

> The construction of a Europe without borders, with its corollary of the approximation of the various national legal systems, including the criminal systems, presupposes that the States involved will be guided by the same values. It is here, in the sphere of values, that the principle under consideration achieves its full significance.[29]

To continue this a little further the opinion stated:

> The *ne bis in idem* principle is not, as I have already pointed out, a procedural rule, but a fundamental safeguard for citizens in legal systems which, like those of the partners of the European Union, are based on the acknowledgement that the individual has a series of rights and freedoms in respect of the acts of public bodies.[30]

What is perhaps most interesting, in this interpretation, of the *ne bis in idem* principle is the extent to which it is explicitly connected to the principle of free movement of persons across the EU as a common area. I do not think that this is simply an attempt to use criminal law to bolster the freedoms of the internal market, rather it demonstrates that a European-wide co-operation on criminal justice matters requires the representation of a common area with a putative single authority concerning the designation of criminal prosecutions. Although the ECJ never explicitly states that the European common area of criminal justice trumps the national interest in pursuing prosecution this is more than implicit in the ECJ's consideration of *ne bis in idem*. This is acknowledged openly by the Commission in the conclusion to the communication document on mutual recognition:

> With the introduction of mutual recognition, the moment appears to have come for the existing system, by which a number of Member States could have jurisdiction for the same offence, to be complemented by rules clearly designating one Member State.[31]

The Commission puts forward a possible resolution to this problem which entails an external body designating which jurisdiction has competence over the criminal matter; one of the candidates for such an oversight position is the AFSJ agency Eurojust:

> Where the rules are not clear with regard to a specific case or where Member States might – for whatever reason – insist on their competence, could it become necessary to refer the issue to a European body for a decision on the jurisdictional

29 Ibid., para. 55.

30 Ibid., para. 114.

31 Ibid., p. 19.

issue. This task could be entrusted to the European Court of Justice, to Eurojust or to a similar body.[32]

It is apparent that surrounding the issue of *ne bis in idem* is not simply a procedural question over the jurisdiction for criminal prosecution but a more complex matter concerning the *representation* of the EU as a common area of criminal justice and also that it is the EU that claims a certain authority over criminal actions taken against individuals. This last aspect concerning the authority to conduct criminal actions against individuals will be even more apparent if the proposal to create a European Prosecutor is passed (the legal basis already exists in the Lisbon Treaty).

The Legitimacy of a Common Area of Criminal Justice

The representation of a common area of criminal justice in the EU coupled with the implied claim to prosecuting authority of the EU institutions also must be viewed in the wider context of the significant enhancement of powers and competences under the Lisbon Treaty which sees the third pillar competences transferred to the 'community' method. The implications of the common area of justice clearly raise profound questions concerning the constitutional legitimacy of these practices. Criminal law, in particular, touches the sovereignty of the state as the ultimate point of coercive authority. Therefore it is to be accepted that the constitutional discussion that has taken place does revolve around the issue of the appropriate site of legitimacy for the common area of criminal justice; does it reside with the EU or the state or a mixture of both? But beyond this question we also have the problem that if a legitimate location can be agreed, how can this be justified in constitutional terms (must it be at all)? Due to the rather limited role that the ECJ has had in providing preliminary references for the third pillar we have not seen the overt constitutional declarations by the ECJ which came to characterise the understanding, and development, of the EC in its early years.[33] Nevertheless there has been a modest 'dialogue' at the level of the national courts (particularly from the *Bundesverfassungsgericht*), and occasionally involving the ECJ, which does explore this fundamental question concerning the constitutional legitimacy of the common area of criminal justice.

The first example of the awareness of a concern over the legitimacy of establishing a common area of justice emerges in the national courts in response to the measures in respect of extradition, the European Arrest Warrant (EAW). It will be recalled that the EAW implemented mutual recognition in criminal justice matters by providing for a common scheme for the extradition of suspects in matters of serious criminal offences. This framework decision is a powerful illustration of the idea of mutual recognition since it abolishes the condition of

32 Ibid., p. 20.

33 For further debate about this, see the relevant sections of Chapter 1.

dual criminality – leading to the possibility that a Member State must extradite a suspect, to another Member State, for conduct carried out in that Member State but which is not necessarily criminal in the domestic jurisdiction. The legitimacy of a common and speedy mutual recognition concerning the procedural and administrative exchange between criminal jurisdictions of the EU, in the absence of common substantive criminal law, was raised by the *Bundesverfassungsgericht* in a judgment of 18 July 2005.[34] The case involved the surrender of a suspect to the Spanish authorities for allegedly being involved in serious terrorist activities. The appellant brought an appeal claim before the Court alleging that the EAW breached fundamental rights under German basic law. The Court allowed the appeal and so refused the extradition of the suspect to Spain; however, this was not on the grounds that the framework decision of the EAW was in breach of German constitutional law but rather that the German enacting law failed to use the margin of appreciation, accorded under in the framework decision, in order to provide adequate protections to the individual subject to extradition procedures.

According to this route it would appear that the Court did *not* openly question the legitimacy and legality of the framework decision itself; in other words, it did not follow the path of the *Solange* litigation which witnessed a direct challenge concerning the level of protection for fundamental rights afforded by the EU.[35] Even so, the decision of the *Bundesverfassungsgericht* does appear to question the constitutional presuppositions underlying mutual recognition and the legitimacy of the common area of criminal justice. Mitsilegas, and others, have pointed out that it is significant that this judgment does not seem to accept the direction of the ECJ in the case of *Pupino*,[36] in which constitutional doctrines developed in the first pillar (indirect effect – interpreting national law in the light of EC legal measures) could be applied in the context of third pillar measures on mutual recognition. The rejection of the attempt to read national legislation in the light of the framework decision, perhaps leads to the view that, 'mutual recognition in criminal matters remains a limited form of integration which is not devoid of (domestic) constitutional checks and balances'.[37] Ultimately, it might be possible to advance the view that for the national constitutional courts mutual recognition is seen as a means of ensuring the continued national identity of the state rather

---

34 *Re Constitutionality of German Law Implementing the Framework Decision on a European Arrest Warrant* [2006] 1 CMLR 16. It is also to be noted that a similar approach to the *Bundesverfassungsgericht* was taken by the Polish Constitutional Tribunal. However, in a somewhat different approach, the Polish Tribunal was prepared to countenance that the Polish Constitution, Article 55(1), be changed so as to ensure compatibility with the framework decision, see Polish Constitutional Tribunal, 27 April 2005, No. P 1/05.

35 *Solange I* [1974] CMLR 540, *Solange II* [1987] 3 CMLR 225, concerning the protection accorded to fundamental rights in EC law.

36 C-105/03 *Pupino* [2005] ECR I-5285.

37 Valsamis Mitsilegas, 'The Transformation of Criminal Law in the Area of Freedom, Security and Justice' at p. 18.

than as a means of furthering the effectiveness of a common area of criminal justice in Europe. The *Bundesverfassungsgericht* recognises that even procedural criminal law can have a profound effect on individual liberty and it is not only important for the national legal order to remain effective supervisors of this but that ultimately the legitimacy of criminal law remains centred in the national constitutional setting (we shall say more about this connection later in response to the judgment of the *Bundesverfassungsgericht* on the Lisbon Treaty).

It is interesting that in the year following the judgment of the German Constitutional Court on the EAW the ECJ obtained a chance to review the application of the EAW itself, and this was against the backdrop of a number of national Constitutional Courts holding that the domestic implementation of the EAW framework decision contravened national constitutional law.[38] In the case of *Advocaten voor de Wereld*[39] the ECJ was asked, by the Constitutional Court of Belgium, to give a preliminary ruling as to whether framework decisions 'may be adopted only for the purpose of approximation of the laws and regulations of the Member States' and secondly whether 'in so far as it (framework Decision) sets aside the verification of the requirement of double criminality for the offences listed therein, compatible with Article 6(2) EU and, more specifically, with the principle of legality in criminal proceedings guaranteed by that provision and with the principle of equality and non-discrimination'. The decision on these matters, by the ECJ, was never in doubt and the overall legality of the framework decision was confirmed. However, what is more interesting is some of the aspects of the judgment concerning harmonisation and the common criminal legal space, which always pose the controversial question: on what basis can a common criminal justice system be justified?

It is the opinion of Advocate General Ruiz-Jarabo Colomer that most interestingly touches on these wider issues and consequently merits close attention. The Advocate General starts his opinion by acknowledging that the framework decision on the arrest warrant has resulted in a far-reaching debate concerning the risk of incompatibility between the Constitutions of Member States and European Union law and remarks that 'the Court of Justice must participate in that debate ... with a view to situating the interpretation of the values and principles which form the foundation of the Community legal system within parameters comparable to the ones which prevail in national systems'.[40] This is a highly suggestive claim which seems to suggest that the EU legal order must develop 'comparable' commitments to the national legal orders in respect of a common area of criminal justice if measures such as the EAW are to stand

38 In particular: Poland, Cyprus, the Czech Republic and France.

39 Case C-303/05 *Advocaten voor de Wereld* [2007] ECR I-3633. Note that by the time this case came before the ECJ a number of Constitutional Courts had questioned the national implementing measures of the framework decision on the Arrest Warrant (Poland, Cyprus and the Czech Republic).

40 Ibid., para, 8.

up to constitutional scrutiny. The key word is of course 'comparable', which opens the way for suggesting that in translating the values and principles of the national legal order to the EU something alters or changes, but this begs more questions than it answers. Turning to the substantive legal issues facing the ECJ the Advocate General draws a clear distinction between the old system of extradition procedure, based around the traditional understanding of the primacy of the sovereign state in the public international legal order, and the view of an arrest warrant scheme which provides the basis for 'assistance and surrender' based on the principle of mutual recognition between the Member States.[41] He states:

> The situation (traditional form of extradition) changes when assistance is requested and provided in the context of a supranational, harmonized legal system where, by partially renouncing their sovereignty, states devolve power to independent authorities with law making power ... the aim is to provide assistance to someone with whom one shares principles, values and objectives.[42]

Here is a clear statement as to the common area of criminal justice to which the principle of mutual recognition becomes the co-ordinating term. What becomes of particular interest to this extent is the use of the term 'partially renouncing their sovereignty', which is employed by the Advocate General in such a way as to echo the terminology of the ECJ in the seminal *Van Gend* case.[43] The words of the Advocate General are again suggestive of an understanding that the common area of justice has led to sovereignty being seceded from the Member States to the EU, but once more this begs the obvious question, what does it really mean to 'renounce sovereignty' in respect of criminal law? Clearly the word 'sovereignty' is being used to cover something important which the Advocate General sees as transformative in the relationship between the EU and Member States but also the very way that co-operation in respect of criminal justice matters is understood.

Whatever the uncertainties over the underlying constitutional legitimacies of the relationship between EU criminal justice measures and the national legal order there seems to be little doubt, in the opinion of Advocate General Colomer, that realisation of the 'aim' of mutual assistance becomes identified strongly with the role of legal officials:

> in that context, inspired by mutual trust, co-operation is based not on the coming together of separate interests but rather on a common provision ... *in other words the political authorities must allow the judicial authorities to take the lead.*[44]

41 Ibid., para. 43.

42 Ibid.

43 C-26/62 *Van Gend en Loos* [1963] ECR 1.

44 Advocate General's opinion in C-303/05 *Advocaten voor den Wereld*, at para. 45.

The legal officials become the arbiters of the scheme not only in individuals' cases but also as to how the common standards and principles, across the common space, are to be observed in actuality (I shall have a little more to say about this in the context of discussing the understanding of 'trust' later in the chapter). This might be construed as an attempt to assuage concerns that the 'sovereignty' exercised on the part of the EU is to be at the detriment of the national legal order, particularly the courts. Indeed it is the partnership of officials across the common space of criminal justice which is to form the basis of how the measures are to function. As far as the EAW measure is concerned, the Advocate General appears to be convinced that in reality the measure does not really threaten the provisions of the national legal orders since it is not intended to be 'punitive' in nature and, in any case, the substantive criminal law of the national legal orders must be robust in the defence of individuals:

> Thus, the certainty required by that principle (*nullum crimen, nulla poena sine lege*) must be demanded from the substantive criminal law of the issuing Member State and, therefore, from the legislature and the courts of that State for the purposes of commencing criminal proceeding ... I must add that the arrest and surrender procedure entailed in the execution of a European arrest warrant is not punitive in nature.[45]

The interest of this judgment stems from the suggestion of deep uncertainty that it conveys over the common area of justice. On the one hand the Advocate General seems relatively certain that the EAW, and mutual recognition, does entail a 'partial reduction of sovereignty', whilst on the other hand reserving a considerable role for the national legal orders in underpinning the functioning of the measure and the safeguards for the individual. What is, perhaps, most redolent of the difficulties in this case is that whilst it is acknowledged, both by the Advocate General and the ECJ itself, that there must be something which supports and confirms the trust necessary for there to be a judicial mutual recognition in a common area of justice, what this might be does not seem forthcoming. The only tentative response made by the Advocate General is the encouragement of assistance between the legal officials who are responsible for administering the common area of justice.

If there seems to be an inability in being able to adequately express the deeper questions as to where the source of legitimacy for criminal justice lies and on what basis can there be a trust in the procedures of mutual recognition it is interesting that such a void has recently been filled by the *Bundesverfassungsgericht.* In a judgment concerning the compatibility of the provisions of the Lisbon Treaty with the German Constitution the *Bundesverfassungsgericht* establish a strong interpretation of the central question of the underlying legitimacy of a common area

45 Ibid., para. 105.

of criminal justice.[46] The judgment is wide-ranging in its scope and it is towards the end of the text that the Court considers the important alterations proposed in the Treaty concerning the AFSJ; and, in particular, the criminal law competences of the EU. The Court is at great pains to emphasise that the compatibility of the criminal law powers of the EU (enhanced as already mentioned above in the Lisbon Treaty) with German Constitutional law can only be sustained if the powers accorded to the EU are interpreted narrowly:

> Due to the fact that democratic self-determination is affected in an especially sensitive manner by provisions of criminal law and criminal procedure, the corresponding basic powers in the treaties must be interpreted strictly – on no account extensively – and their use requires particular justification.[47]

The court adopted such a view because their premise is that the democratic credentials of criminal law are tied to the nation state, and therefore the legitimacy of any integration in respect of criminal justice must be interpreted narrowly (i.e. by reference to the legitimacy stemming from the state). Such an approach is most clearly apparent in the following extract from the judgment:

> Democratic self-determination is, however, affected in a particularly sensitive manner where a legal community is prevented from deciding on the punishability of conduct, or even the imposition of prison sentences, according to their own values. This applies all the more the closer these values are connected with historical experience, traditions of faith and other factors essential to the self-esteem of the people and their society. In these areas, it is therefore only permitted to a limited extent to transfer the competence for criminal legislation, and it is at any rate necessary to comply with the requirements placed on a single act of transfer of a sovereign power (Article 23.1 second sentence of the Basic Law) if the list of areas of crime which fall under the competence of Union legislation is extended.[48]

Interestingly the Court also indicates that as an aspect of this narrow interpretation of the criminal law competences of the EU values and traditions of thought from the State (German) tradition of criminal law could be read into the emerging criminal law *acquis* of the EU. In the following passage the court argue that any criminal law of the EU ought to be premised around the 'guilt' of the 'free will' of the individual which is enshrined in the Basic Law of the German Constitution.

---

46 2/08 *Gauweiler v Treaty of Lisbon.* The English version of the judgment of the Constitutional Court can be found on the Court's website: http://www.bundesverfassungsgericht.de/entscheidungen/es20090630_2bve000208en.html

47 Ibid., para. 358.

48 Ibid., para. 363.

> Moreover, the competences of the European Union in the area of the administration of criminal law must be interpreted in a way that complies with the requirements of the principle of guilt. Criminal law is based on the principle of guilt. This principle presupposes a human being's own responsibility, it presupposes human beings who themselves determine their actions and can decide in favour of right or wrong by virtue of their freedom of will. The protection of human dignity is based on the idea of Man as a spiritual and moral being which has the capabilities of defining himself, and of developing, in freedom.[49]

The *Bundesverfassungsgericht* decision does reflect a version of the legitimacy question which, not unsurprisingly, puts the constitutional state at the universal centre of a possible explanatory account of the legitimate roots of criminal law. However, what becomes more significant about the judgment of the *Bundesverfassungsgericht* is that if you strip away the references to state legitimacy what the Court presupposes is a fundamental relationship between the criminal law and democracy (understood broadly as participation in a political community). To some extent the Court seems to place this as an ontological condition of the criminal law – to think about crime and punishment is to think about the nature of political involvement, belonging and the very protection of that order. Of course, it is usual to use the state as a shorthand answer to these questions but an EU criminal law makes the use of this shorthand all the more difficult as we are, almost by necessity, to pose deeper questions about the political order of the EU. I consider that this observation gives clarity to the words used by Advocate General Colomer, in the *Advocaten* case, that values and principles form the foundation of the community legal system 'within parameters comparable to the ones which prevail in the national legal system'. 'Comparable' here refers to the way that to think about criminal justice measures is inevitably to consider the nature of political involvement and this is something that was recognised by the *Bundesverfassungsgericht*.

In our consideration of the concerns over what is the basis of the assertion that the common area of justice in Europe must be a trust we have reached a certain generality; the trust that exists, and that also underpins the constitutional legitimacy of the criminal justice integration, must be to do with a political involvement or democracy. However, as with the Lisbon case the *Bundesverfassungsgericht* chooses to think about this relationship by employing the familiar conceptual category of the 'nation state'. It is a principal contention, throughout this book, that if we are really to face the constitutional legitimacy concerns raised by the AFSJ then we must force ourselves to think beyond the convenient conceptual categories and to confront the meaning of what is taking place. As I have emphasised, such a confrontation is as much a practical engagement with those practices as a reflection upon them, the crucial point being that we must not 'hide' from the radical nature of the questions posed by what is happening. Perhaps, in this instance, the radical question is how might we consider that a common

49 Ibid., para. 364.

area of criminal justice implicates the political such that we invoke a language of democracy and political participation? Such a question may always seem strange precisely because it is always in flux and shifting according to the continuing changes in our traditions of understanding this question. We cannot expect to achieve a settled explanatory account but must engage with it in order to reveal how it can be meaningful to the possibilities that we have concerning the future. What is crucial is that we are able to preserve the strangeness of it as a question. Taking something of a different direction from the consideration of the practices of the AFSJ, the legal philosopher René Foqué provides a most thoughtful reflection on this question and one that may highlight what I have been trying to suggest about the idea of 'trust' in the common area of justice.

René Foqué observes that it is the tensions over the relationship between the criminal law and the political order that occupy a philosophical approach to criminal law.[50] In the 'relational conception' of criminal law Foqué advocates an awareness of the 'open-texture' concerning the interpretative relationship between the norms of the criminal law and the commitments[51] of the political community.[52] Such a nexus between the orientations provided by the common commitments of a political community and the criminal law fundamentally exists for Foqué because of the unique place of the individual as a participant, and deliberator, in the common commitments of the community – which recognises human dignity as an aspect of the fragility of the human condition.[53]

In an effort to convey the tensions in the relationship, or as I put it to preserve the strangeness of the relationship between the political order and the criminal law, Foqué draws upon the Greek dramatic text of the *Oresteia* by Aeschylus. Written in Athens at the beginning of the 'golden age' of the fifth century BC, three plays dramatise the fortunes of Atreus from the dark beginnings of murder to the light of Athenian democracy in the final play. Clearly the resort to such a text becomes a way of thinking afresh about the relationship, in the present, and of indicating certain possibilities and limitations without the necessity of expressing these in familiar conceptual terms.

The trilogy opens at the end of the war with Troy with the triumphant return of the King Agamemnon to Argos. The joy of return is short lived, however, as Agamemnon's wife, Clytaemnestra, murders her husband for the sacrifice of their daughter, Iphigenia, and the taking of Cassandra as a mistress. In the second play, Orestes avenges the death of his father by murdering his mother Clytaemnestra, thus committing the offence of matricide, and so is pursued by the Furies, the Gods who guard the sacred blood-ties of the family. The final play sees Orestes pursued by the Furies to the city of Athens where he is committed to the Goddess Athena

50 René Foqué, 'Criminal Justice in a Democracy: Towards a Relational Conception of Criminal Law and Punishment', 2 *Criminal Law and Philosophy* (2008), pp. 207–227.

51 Foqué uses the term 'value-orientations'.

52 Ibid., p. 223.

53 Ibid., p. 224.

for her judgment. Athena establishes the jury of citizens, the *Areopagus*, to decide over the fate of Orestes. Hearing the speeches of both Orestes and the Furies the *Areopagus* votes to acquit Orestes and restore him to his ancestral lands in Argos. The Furies, angered by a decision which abandons the primitive vendetta-laws of blood-ties, threaten to destroy the city of Athens. However, Athena persuades the Furies to be transformed into the exalted guardians of the city, the *polis*, and to protect its bonds of civil governance; they become the *Eumenides* (the kindly ones). The final chorus is a hymn to this new order in the city of Athens and the transformation from the bloody vendettas of the first play to the era of justice and order is complete.

The narrative of the play is one of transformation; the first two plays contain a cyclical violence which threatens the most sacred ties of blood and family in such a manner that there seems to be little scope for resolution. The human agents in the drama are also 'caught' for the primitive cycle of vengeance is undertaken by the relentless presence of the Gods, and in particular, the Furies. The final play opens a dialectic in which the violent murders are avenged not through a counter-act of violence but by the capacity for reconciliation and the co-operation of the community. In this respect it is noteworthy that at the decisive moment it is Athena who passes agency over determining the course of events to the 'finest men of Athens to Judge', acknowledging that if justice is to be achieved then this entails the participation of individuals and the necessary political ties, represented by the institution of the *Areopagus*, and protected by the Kindly Ones.

The relationship between the political order and criminal justice appears in this play as a foundational journey out of the primitive and mythical blood-feud. However, at the heart of the play, and the issue which is of central to the concern of the present chapter, is the question of the political trust which is necessary to orientate the political community towards the just criminal order. René Foqué summarises this dilemma arising out of the *Oresteia*:

> [The *Oresteia*] provides us with a theatrical representation of the consequences of this political, legal and anthropological process as to the relevance of criminal law in the democratic order. Matricide violates the most fundamental values held by humanity, and therefore it constitutes an evil for which there can be no redemption ... That question asks how the ability of a community to co-operate and its capacity for self-institutionalisation can be repaired.[54]

The common area of criminal justice implies the resilient commitment to, and trust in, the political order by which a community copes and reconciles itself to the acts of violence that are perpetrated. What if the criminal law does not possess such a relationship to the political order? Whilst this question lies beyond the immediate remit of this book and, therefore, can perhaps be viewed as conjecture, it is suggestive that criminal justice does seem to relate to the legitimacy of

54 Ibid., p. 212.

constitutional life such that the act of punishment (and forgiveness) forms part of how we relate our common commitments to each other. Without this, criminal law may become the technical and methodical act of imposing coercion upon one another and so, in the extreme form, may not be capable of revealing any meaning.

It is interesting that many of the concerns that are developed at the more philosophical level by René Foqué are echoed by the constitutional theorist Klaus Günther in an article which considers the implications of the security discourse upon our understanding of the relationship between the political order and criminal law. Günther argues that in the climate of post-9/11 criminal law has expanded such that it is 'only spoken of in connection with internal security'.[55] Not only does this have the effect of causing the dissolution of established or stable legal understandings; for example, concerning the legal status of terrorist prisoners at Guantánamo Bay detention camp, but equally it distorts the very sense that we have of freedom under the law.[56] Günther's views echo, albeit in a reverse sense, the plays of the *Oresteia* because the most real threat to freedom is when the criminal act of violence becomes uncoupled from a connection with the basis of a common political community. Günther identifies such a threat to the relationship between criminal law and democracy through the practices of security.

Turning attention back to the practices of the AFSJ it can be asked in what sense, if at all, have the dominant practices of security enforced a distinction between the criminal law and the political? What seems genuinely interesting about this question, in the EU context, is that in relation to criminal justice it would seem that the question of the importance of political community or the democratic basis of criminal law is not something that is ignored or unacknowledged. This can be witnessed from the doctrines of European criminal law which place the values of 'mutual recognition' and 'trust' at the core of how criminal justice must appeal to something held in common. There is also awareness that 'trust' must mean ways of uncovering of the conditions of political and democratic trust and as such the practices of criminal justice play into the deeply-rooted problems of how to understand a democratic political community 'beyond' the nation state. In the most recent policy document concerning the AFSJ, the Stockholm Programme (2009), there is evidence of an increasing sense of the importance of the connection between democratic participation, rights and criminal justice; for instance, in the midst of paragraphs concerning measures to build upon criminal justice there is also an invitation for the Commission to consider 'participation in the democratic life of the Union'.[57] It is indeed encouraging to find such a concern in this document and it will be necessary to follow how such proposals develop in time. Perhaps the policy document of the Stockholm Programme does offer some indication of an

55 Klaus Günther, 'World Citizens between Freedom and Security', 12(3) *Constellations* (2005), pp. 379–391 at p. 381.

56 Ibid., p. 384.

57 Council of the European Union, 'Stockholm Programme – An open and secure Europe serving and protecting the citizens' at para. 2.6.

awareness of the deeper difficulties when freedom, security and justice measures become free from constitutional consideration surrounding questions over the meaning and involvement of political community. To this extent Stockholm may be seen as offering an opening, or window, towards constitutional thinking. Nevertheless, in stating this we must be cautious as it is apparent that further varieties of thinking may suggest that 'trust' can also be construed in such a way that departs from the constitutional and draws instead upon an instrumentalism concerning the place of 'trust' in the common area of criminal justice.

It will be recalled that the central doctrine of mutual recognition is said to rely upon a notion of 'trust'. In various policy documents which attempt to outline the meaning of 'trust' it is possible to find a meaning which accords to 'trust' the idea of a value which makes the system 'operational'. For example, consider the following extract from one such document:

> Mutual trust is an important element, not only trust in the adequacy of one's partners' rules, but also that these rules are correctly applied. Based on this idea of equivalence and the trust it is based on, the results the state has reached are allowed to take into effect in one's own sphere of legal influence.[58]

The operative features of trust can be clearly detected in the last sentence of this quote in which trust becomes a notion of 'equivalence' in the operation of the different legal systems. However, it is the phrase 'to take into effect in one's own sphere of legal influence' that seems most interesting as it appears to be directed at someone: we might ask whose sphere of legal influence does this sort of understanding of trust refer to? Clues might be found if we return to the comments of Advocate General Colomer in *Advocaten voor de Wereld*, where he commented that:

> in that context, inspired by mutual trust, co-operation is based not on the coming together of separate interests but rather on a common provision ... *in other words the political authorities must allow the judicial authorities to take the lead.*[59]

It is in the phrase 'the political authorities must allow the judicial authorities to take the lead' that we encounter the person to whom operational trust refers – the judicial authorities. Casting the net wider it is clear that a number of concrete measures have either been passed or are currently being contemplated so as to ensure that 'trust' is made operational by the legal authorities. One example of this is the body set up called the European Judicial Network,[60] which is set up to aid co-operation between the 'judicial authorities' of Member States in respect of criminal matters. The

58 COM (2000) 495 (final), 'Mutual Recognition of Final Decisions in Criminal matters', p. 4.

59 Advocate General's opinion in C-303/05 *Advocaten voor den Wereld*, at para. 45.

60 See Joint Action adopted by the Council, 98/428/JHA on the creation of a judicial network, OJ L 191.

Network operates by establishing 'operational contact points' in various Member States, which seems to be a way of facilitating inter-personal relations between officials, periodic meetings or gatherings of officials and up-to-date information (a telecommunications network).[61] In the most recent policy documents to outline the long-term course of the AFSJ, the Stockholm Programme, it is interesting to observe that the Council recommends that 'to foster a genuine judicial and law enforcement culture, it is essential to step up training on EU related issues and to make it systematically accessible for all professions involved in the implementation of the AFSJ'.[62] This training of officials involves the possibility of common European training schemes; joint courses, exercises and exchange programmes including an 'Erasmus' style exchange programme for judges.[63] In addition to developing a supportive and co-operative network, including specific training measures, there is also a role in fostering mutual trust to be played by some of the professional agencies which belong to the AFSJ. An example is Eurojust which functions as a liaison point between the different agencies of the AFSJ on criminal justice matters, such as Europol, Frontex and the Member States.[64]

Whilst it is inevitable that there will be an operational dimension to the idea of mutual recognition supported by trust the danger is that such operational considerations, or needs, simply eclipse the more complex and difficult understanding of political trust. In other words, the deep constitutional sense of 'trust' needed to found a relationship between criminal law and the political becomes replaced by an understanding that 'trust' is something that can be delivered in terms of the operation of the system of mutual recognition. This operational approach can be located even within the terms of the new Lisbon Treaty where there is a troubling indication that a common area of justice may not be a space for genuine political involvement capable of sustaining trust and the democratic foundation of the criminal sanction, but rather instead meet the operational and technical delivery of security. In Article 71 TFEU explicit mention is made of the intention to ensure that Member States can co-operate, within the framework of the EU, to augment the delivery of internal security as an *operational* good:

> A standing committee shall be set up within the Council in order to ensure that operational cooperation on internal security is promoted and strengthened within the Union ... representatives of the bodies, offices and agencies of the Union concerned may be involved in the proceedings of this committee.

---

61 Joint Action 98/428/JHA, ibid., Article 3.

62 Council of the European Union, 'Stockholm Programme – An open and secure Europe serving and protecting the citizens', at p. 9.

63 Ibid.

64 For the account of the powers of the agency Eurojust, see Council Decision 2002/187/JHA. Additionally, see Council Decision 2009/426 for proposals on new powers for Eurojust in respect of initiation of investigations and resolving conflicts of competence between the Member States.

Whilst it is true that this article pronounces that the European Parliament and national Parliaments 'shall be kept informed of the proceedings', it would seem to be a limited concession and one which also falls within the classical restraint view of constitutionalism.

It is difficult to extrapolate an entire attitude towards these very complex relationships between criminal justice, trust, political community and democracy on the basis of a single article in the Treaty. However, it does at least point to the need for caution. The understanding of criminal justice as simply a facet of operational internal security constitutes the danger of disconnecting criminal justice from the political; such an implication would risk making the violence exercised by, and in the name of, the collective literally meaningless. More than any other dimension of policy in the AFSJ it is criminal justice which must bring to our attention the importance of constitutional thinking.

Conclusion

The trajectory of this chapter has been to indicate the deep questions of constitutional legitimacy and political trust which are engaged by a establishing a common area of criminal justice. The criminal law exists in a close relation to the common commitments of the political community, and therefore reinforce the sense of agency in the source of legitimate authority. It is this close connection to the legitimacy of the political community which the *Bundesverfassungsgericht* acknowledges in its interpretation of the criminal justice policy of the AFSJ. The *Bundesverfassungsgericht* may limit its analysis to the conventional conception of the state but justifiably indicates that a common space of criminal justice in Europe does raise deep issues of political trust and legitimacy which go to the core of the concerns about the constitutionality of an area of common criminal justice. The challenge posed is not to neglect this dimension of the criminal justice features of the AFSJ and to constantly engage imaginatively in what such practices may mean. I considered the work of René Foqué precisely to indicate the ways unfamiliar texts may be points of imaginative reflection so as to consider the relationship of criminal law to political authority outside the horizons of our conventional conceptual categories and language.

Chapter 7
Conclusion: Learning Constitutionalism

Introduction

This book has attempted to make the language and thinking of 'constitutionalism' important to an understanding of the development of policy concerning internal security in the European Union's area of freedom, security and justice. Above all, constitutionalism has been presented as a challenge, or indeed, a way of confronting, how we are going about this political endeavour in the European context and that it is the commitment to constitutional thinking which must be crucial if the AFSJ can be free, just *and* secure. At present the European Union sits at something of a crossroads in these aspects. The last years have seen an encroaching tide of measures and technological procedures intended to bolster the perception that the EU takes seriously the security challenges facing us in the twenty-first century. Whilst such a programme is, perhaps, inevitable it also places the EU in a certain predicament. It has already been developed, in this book, that security is a public good which is highly problematical since it perpetuates a fundamental paradox in the activity of governing. This paradox, and the difficulty that this poses for the AFSJ, become central to the constitutional challenges that the EU encounters. At root the EU employs an understanding of security that is intended to offer the basis, or grounding, for the constitutional legitimacy of the activities of the AFSJ. Such a reliance upon a highly instrumental notion of security, as a facet of the techniques of governing, exhibits the capacity to distort how we are able to think about the constitutional meaning of a common area of justice or of freely moving across the common borders of the EU.

The constitutional difficulties surrounding the AFSJ are not straightforwardly addressed; the pervasiveness of instrumental thinking surrounding our constitutional lives (as illustrated by Chapters 3 and 4) entails that it is not an easy matter to suggest that what is required are more measures which have their goal as seeking to guarantee freedom or to provide enhanced protection for individuals. Without addressing ourselves to what is truly question-worthy in our constitutional life and how we can foster a language of constitutional thinking, such an appeal to freedom, or the protection of individuals, can easily form part of the very techniques of governing that conceal or distort constitutional life. For this reason it was always a central concern that a constitutional inquiry into the practices of the AFSJ must reveal that the very conventions as to how we have approached constitutionalism must be called into question. In fact, in this final chapter, I would like to concentrate on precisely this issue; the implications for the area of freedom, security and justice are not to be contained in a raft of policy proposals, objectives and measures but rather by the ability to reinvigorate and augment a language of constitutionalism by which we can *confront the meaning* of territory, authority, belonging, participation and the commitments for the sake of which we come together as political peoples. In this chapter I argue that what is most essential about constitutionalism is precisely not to impose a conceptual or theoretical template upon these questions, which risks distorting or concealing the fundamental basis of the ways of constitutional life, but instead to understand how we can learn to acknowledge a way to keep and foster the activity of constitutional life as open-ended. Only by setting ourselves upon this more challenging path towards constitutional thinking will we reveal the particular problems that we encounter in the practices of criminal justice, free movement, and so forth, in circumstances where we have come to acknowledge that the nation state no longer provides the conceptual grid (if ever it did) with which to settle questions of constitutional legitimacy.

In short, the task of this book, and consequently its implications for the AFSJ and the wider EU, has not been the construction, and imposition, of a public philosophy capable of providing some grounding, or foundation, for a sphere of politics credited as going beyond the historical and institutional trajectory of the nation state in matters of security policy. Indeed, the fundamental task has been for constitutionalism not to be called forth as a public philosophy. The essential value of constitutionalism does not lie in becoming a tool to be employed to bring about ready-to-hand justifications for the political order but rather to reveal the essential dimensions of our constitutional life and the necessity for our involvement with all attentiveness to this task. In the course of this chapter I would like to reflect on the nature of such a task by exploring the kind of involvement this entails.

Deepening our Constitutional Involvement

Responding to the claim that the EU possesses an autonomous public sphere, or an independent source of sovereignty from the nation state tends to become the principal concern and primary task for constitutional theorists in the EU. As I considered in Chapter 1, the constitutional task, as conventionally perceived, presents two problems: grappling with the epistemological problem of being able to know that there is a EU public sphere (and, therefore, the institutional dynamics of its existence) and, secondly, searching for some normative grounding for this emerging public space. The extent to which constitutionalism tends to circle around these two endeavours indicates the extent to which our thinking has become slavishly bound to categories and concepts, and primary amongst these is the concept of a sovereign entity possessing a public legitimised by the representation of a people. Why have we become so concerned with this?

The fixation with the constitutional mechanics of the public sphere derives from a historical transition from the hierarchical model of theological Kingship, of the middle ages, to the emergence of secular states with an ascending notion of authority derived from the 'people'[1] – a movement which first began in the Renaissance cities of the Italian Peninsula and which gradually spread throughout Europe and to America. The rules and procedures of constitutionalism, which in Chapter 2 I termed the 'restraint' view of constitutionalism, were intended to provide the rules and mechanisms to guarantee that the public space would remain autonomous (that is, not to succumb to tyranny) and by doing so could ensure the conditions of our democratic participation in preserving an ascending account of authority.

In the EU it is apparent that whatever the concerns (of some constitutional theorists) about granting the EU an autonomous public sphere, policy documents and Treaty provisions clearly give great weight to the importance of fostering and augmenting the constitutional rules, procedures and institutions designed to ensure the integrity of the EU public sphere. Such a turn to constitutionalism must be intended to resolve, or settle, the question over the *legitimacy* of the EU as an entity which claims a sovereign public sphere. Concerns about the constitutional legitimacy of the EU are characterised by debates, at European and national level, concerning the quality of democratic decision making and the participatory involvement of EU nationals in the activity of governing; a debate often referred to as the 'democratic deficit'.

The extent to which we may be concerned about the *legitimacy* of that which is taking place in the EU, including the important policy considered here concerning internal security, has ensured that constitutionalism has been called upon to seek solutions and enhance both the mechanisms through which power can be said to be restrained as well as to ensure our involvement in government. Constitutionalism becomes the vernacular of thinking about the basis upon which European political authority must be *founded*. Despite the recent failure of efforts to compose a constitutional document (the Constitutional Treaty) to resolve the challenges of democratic and constitutional legitimacy of the EU the most recent reforms, in the Treaty of Lisbon, witness a renewed vigour for constitutional answers to the problems of the European public sphere.

Glancing at the principal features and innovations of the Lisbon Treaty it is impossible to neglect those aspects which appear to stem from a concern about the constitutional legitimacy of the European public sphere. Article 294 TFEU contains provisions concerning the 'ordinary' procedure by which European law is to be made. It is a procedure which gives an important role to the European Parliament to formally agree, or even veto, measures which are proposed by the Commission. For some time the European Parliament was second fiddle to the interests of the Member States represented by the Council – following Lisbon it has equal voice in the vast majority of fields in European law, including many of those of AFSJ policy. The constitutional notion of 'representation' has been

1 Walter Ullman, *A History of Political Thought in the Middle Ages* (Harmondsworth: Penguin Books, 1965); and also see Charles Taylor, *The Secular Age* (London: The Belknap Press of Harvard University, 2007).

enhanced by augmenting the legislative power of the Parliament as the institution which is thought to represent the peoples' interests, but equally, the Treaty of Lisbon has considered the democratic importance of 'civic participation'. Article 10(3) and 11 TEU contain important commitments to the role played by citizens in the forging of a democratic and constitutional culture:

> Every citizen shall have the right to participate in the democratic life of the Union. Decisions shall be taken as openly and as closely as possible to the citizen.[2]

Such a commitment culminates in an important right of initiative which is no doubt intended to provide a concrete basis for participatory democracy in the EU:

> Not less than one million citizens who are nationals of a significant number of Member States may take the initiative of inviting the European Commission, within the framework of its powers, to submit any appropriate proposal on matters where citizens consider that a legal act of the Union is required for the purpose of implementing the Treaties.[3]

Clearly this goes beyond the symbolism of participation and offers something seemingly actual, although, whether it is employed in practice, or how circumscribed it proves to be, are to be awaited. Finally, in respect of the protection accorded to the rights of the citizen (both political and social) the Lisbon Treaty has provided a formal legal status to the Charter of Fundamental Rights of the European Union.[4]

The movement, witnessed by Lisbon, towards improving the commitment to representational and participatory democracy clearly impacts upon the study of the AFSJ. With the incorporation of the entire policy field of the AFSJ into the common legislative method, once called the 'community method', it is now open for all aspects of internal security policy to benefit from greater awareness of the democratic processes and mechanisms which can enhance citizen participation and protection. To that extent the Stockholm Programme, as I discussed in the previous chapter, can be seen to place more emphasis on the place of democratic participation and constitutional safeguards. This may suggest a shift from the security dominated concerns of previous years (notably in the Hague Programme). Nevertheless, as pointed out over the previous two chapters, in the course of discussing the actual practices of the AFSJ, the idea of security as a technique of government is also deeply rooted in the understanding and tradition of governing and power and the traces of this can be clearly discerned in the AFSJ. Whilst this tempers the optimism that we may have about the political course of the AFSJ, and

2 The text of Article 10(3) TEU.

3 The text of Article 11(4) TEU.

4 This is subject to the amendments negotiated by Poland, the UK and the Czech Republic which are contained in the Protocols to the Lisbon Treaty.

the wider EU, it need not diminish it. However, it is concerning this central sense of optimism in the future orientation of AFSJ, the EU, and the relationship with constitutionalism that must become worthy of further thought.

Throughout this book I have referred to the words 'involvement' or 'participation' in order to convey the sense that constitutionalism entails each of us 'taking up' the question of political activity so as to attain a notion of freedom. Can it be said, therefore, that the measures taken towards strengthening democracy, including that of the participation of citizens, provide a basis for approaching the concerns we have long held over the constitutional legitimacy of the EU? My answer to this question, based on the position I have adopted in this book, would be in so far as we address ourselves to 'constitutional legitimacy' then no – these measures do not directly assist us. This, however, does not mean that I consider the concern to improve participatory democracy, or constitutional restraint and protection, to be 'wrong', 'misplaced' or 'damaging'. I do not mean that I am 'critical' of conventional approaches to constitutionalism in this easy way. What I do advance, in particular in Chapter 2, is the view that the conventional ways, or tools, that we have to consider constitutional legitimacy still do not approach the needs of this task. Why is it the more we devise constitutional methods, procedures, rights, institutions to resolve the problem of constitutional legitimacy the more question-begging the issue of constitutional legitimacy becomes?

Attempting to think about constitutional legitimacy entails that we are open to a new way of thinking, in particular, that we are prepared to abandon the concepts or categories by which we have conventionally thought about constitutional legitimacy through notions of 'authority' and 'identity'. In Chapter 2 the questions of 'authority' and 'identity' become involved in a distinctive mode of deliberation, or thinking, in which constitutional legitimacy is revealed as addressing the common commitments of a political community enfolded over time. This, however, is not an exercise in objective historical determination but rather a situational judgement (*phronēsis*). Drawing upon the work of Hans-Georg Gadamer we can say that the basis for this situational judgement, which reveals how our constitutional commitments guide us in action,[5] is hermeneutic. Furthermore, the essential character of this hermeneutic approach to our constitutional practices is that it reveals something deep about how the common commitments are taken up by us as fundamental to the way we make sense of the each other as a common political community. In other words, the kind of hermeneutic thinking to which I refer is 'ontological'. It is to convey the relationship between the common constitutional commitments of political community, hermeneutic thinking and ontology (existence) that I use the term *constitutional life*. It is by learning how to involve ourselves in constitutional

5 As 'guides' to action this is similar to the position adopted by Michael Oakeshott in his account of 'adverbial considerations'; see, *On Human Conduct* (Oxford: Clarendon Press, 1990).

life that it is possible to cultivate a nearness to constitutional legitimacy. This 'learning' to recognise and cultivate constitutional life must become an urgent question particularly in respect of the EU – the idea that we must 'learn' about our involvement in constitutional life is a matter to think about in the next section of this chapter.

Having, therefore, briefly restated why it is that involvement, or participation, must be thought about differently if we are to approach the problem of constitutional legitimacy I would like to return to the important question – namely, what makes this different from the conventional view of constitutional participation? I stated earlier that I did not intend to advance a view that was 'critical' of the established view of constitutionalism, nor did I consider that the steps taken towards participatory democracy and protection of civic rights could be viewed as 'mistaken' or 'misplaced'. This is in part because I view such actions as displaying a *concerned awareness* towards constitutional legitimacy and, therefore, offering a way of beginning along the path towards thinking about constitutional life. However, I also consider that there are perils or even dangers to assuming that our concerns about constitutional legitimacy can be *resolved* by concepts, mechanisms, procedures or institutions which seek to protect and maintain the 'autonomous' public sphere. Is such a reference to 'perils' or 'dangers' too dramatic? What great peril can there be in sensible measures taken to improve the quality of democracy decision making or the protection of freedoms that we take to be fundamental or universal? The danger is that we think that the complexity of constitutional life can be reduced to a procedure, set of institutions or concepts that are within our technical control or which can be delivered to us by will. In other words, the richness of our constitutional life is concealed as it is turned into a 'standing reserve'[6] for the needs of belonging and identification. I explored this peril to constitutionalism as 'instrumentalism' in Chapter 3. The difficulty is that instrumentalism knows no limitations on its capacity to seek solutions to the delivery of need and in such a situation distorts our ability to think about the constitutional dimensions to our lives. The pervasive influence of instrumentalism is most keenly acknowledged in the diminishing of our resources of language capable of expressing and bringing into being the dimensions of constitutional life.

It is with the commitment, or good, of security that the conflict between instrumental and constitutional understandings comes most clearly into view. Security becomes the good which is most essential to the needs of the political

6 This is a term from an essay by Martin Heidegger, 'The Question concerning Technology' in *Basic Writings*, in which standing reserve or *Bestand* becomes the concealment of modern technology: 'What kind of unconcealment is it, then, that is to that which results from this setting-upon that challenges? Everywhere everything is ordered to stand by, to be immediately on hand, indeed to stand just so that it may be on call for a further ordering. Whatever is ordered about in this way has its own standing. We call it standing reserve [*Bestand*]', p. 322.

community; the sense of or feeling of being secure, belonging as a population and the integrity of the territorial possession are the most vital matters for any work of governing. It is this intention to deliver the security needs of a population that has witnessed the rise of an apparatus or technique of government, a practice Michel Foucault termed 'governmentality'. However, in so far as we crave for such practices to fulfil our need for security then the risk is run that our constitutional life is fundamentally obscured by the instrumental techniques of security. The risks posed by an instrumental understanding of security become particularly problematical for the EU as the area of freedom, security and justice places the temptation to rely on this sense of security as a means of delivering the sense of political community (territory and identification) that would legitimise the practices of integration themselves. I explored, in the previous two chapters, the extent to which an instrumental understanding of security has already obscured the constitutional thinking that is urgently needed if the integration taking place in the AFSJ is to be part of a constitutional life.

It is the task of deepening and questioning our understanding of what involvement or participation *is* which in turn compels us towards recognising the dimensions of constitutional life. However, this raises the obvious query: how are we to acknowledge or 'improve' the way we think about constitutional life? This is a very difficult question. To begin with we cannot expect that improving our way of thinking about constitutional life necessarily will give something in return; therefore, it is not subject to questions such as: 'what is its use?', or 'what is its impact or implication?'. A desire for answers of this sort will lead out of the domain of constitutional thinking and towards instrumentality. Nevertheless I do think it is legitimate to ask: how can we learn about constitutional life? It is this relationship between learning and constitutional life that will be become crucial for any future study of constitutional thinking.

Learning Constitutional Life

In the 1950s the English philosopher and political theorist, Michael Oakeshott, wrote that: 'the expression political education has fallen on evil days; in the wilful and disingenuous corruption of language which is characteristic of our time it has acquired a sinister meaning'.[7] The same would be true also of our times in which the relationship between education or learning and constitutionalism is either presumed to be some kind of ideological indoctrination or the mundane content of citizenship classes. What is at stake in the relationship between education and our political way of life is not a technique or content but the disposition to be involved in the very activity of collective life. The intimate connection between learning and constitutional life has become neglected and it becomes the essential

7 Michael Oakeshott, 'Political Education' in *Rationalism in Politics and Other Essays* (Indianapolis: Liberty Fund, 1991), p. 44.

task for constitutional thinkers to begin to re-think this connection. In the space remaining in this chapter I would like to offer some tentative suggestions towards reinvigorating such a relationship; however, rather than being definitive this is simply intended to be a prologue, or a call, for further reflection.

In coming to a reassessment of the question concerning constitutional legitimacy this book has outlined a view of interpretation which draws heavily on the tradition of hermeneutics in the human sciences developed by Hans-Georg Gadamer in the 1960s. Drawing on the work of his teacher, the philosopher Martin Heidegger, Gadamer sought to make fundamental ontology, or the question of 'being' (*Dasein*), central to the endeavour of the interpretation of meaning. Emerging out of Gadamer's contribution is a very different way of thinking about 'understanding', and by implication also learning, which can be found in the elements of the hermeneutic experience. Three key elements form part of the hermeneutic account; firstly, understanding involves a transformation of experience; secondly, understanding is not about the application of a technique but a situational response (judgement) which takes place in language; and thirdly, attentiveness to language takes place within a dialogue or conversion with another.

Above all, central to the three elements of the hermeneutic experience is that understanding is never given to a 'subject' as if by right or by acquisition. For authentic learning to take place the 'subject' must accept that this involves a change, or transformation, in which comportment to the world is undergone. This fundamental change is ontological in that it implicates the comportment of each being-subject towards that which is experienced in life itself. The medium of this transformation is language itself – and a concern for language is a deep concern about the very possibility for this moment of learning to occur. But even here we risk assuming that our expression of 'language' does not itself undergo this transformation of thinking and understanding with us. For in learning about (constitutional) life we require our language to deepen and open this place to which a new horizon of understanding is taken. Gadamer, following the work of Martin Heidegger, calls this the 'process of poetizing':

> Heidegger asserts that the essence of art is the process of poeticizing. What he means is that the nature of art does not consist in transforming something that is already in being. Rather, art is the project by which something new comes forth as true. The essence of the event of truth that is present in the work of art is that 'it opens up an open place'[8]

This movement to the open possibilities of the 'open place' Gadamer emphasises is something that must come out of the already existing possibilities of language, that is to say the tradition of our understanding:

8 Ibid., p. 228.

> In fact, the process of poeticizing is divided into two phases: into the project that has already occurred where a language holds sway, and another project that allows the new poetic creation to come forth from the first project.[9]

The path towards acknowledging the debt to language is to realise the new possibilities of thinking about constitutional life that can only take place in the midst of language. It is the process of poeticizing that enables us to place limitations on the advance of instrumental thinking in constitutional lives but also to authentically express, and respond to, the different demands of collective commitments, such as those emerging through practices in the EU, and the area of freedom, security and justice. The language of constitutional life must be fostered and developed not by turning to instrumental delivery but by learning new forms of possibility about being together through the process of poeticizing.

The relationship between learning, hermeneutics and constitutional life takes on an element of confrontation. If we are to be transformed in understanding so that new horizons of possibility are to be revealed, in language, then this demands a certain disposition on our part. It requires that we approach learning about constitutional life in a certain way if we are to be successful in our endeavour. What, therefore, might be the conditions of involvement in which we learn about the meaning of our common commitments over time?

Certainly if we are to learn about an involvement which is capable of sustaining both a non-instrumental encounter with each other and of revealing the traditions of our common commitments over time then this is likely to appear to be very different from the qualities and aspects of knowledge we value currently in coming to understand our constitutional arrangements. This has, however, been the principal difficulty throughout this book: just how do we confront the strangeness of trying to consider a very different mode of thinking concerning our constitutional and political practices? In the following account I intend to provide an indication of the practical disposition that may condition how we approach the task of learning about constitutional life.

Firstly, stemming from the elements of the hermeneutic experience, there must be an acknowledgment that learning about constitutional life is not an activity of acquiring and then subsequently applying a technique. Learning is the acceptance of a relationship in which what we are seeking to understand changes us: learning, in this sense, is a practical act of *transformation* which involves comportment towards how we are living. The fundamental basis of this relationship is through language, and throughout this book we have explored the centrality of attentiveness to language as a prerequisite towards understanding and expression between each other, as the dimensions of our common constitutional life. In short, there can be no learning or understanding without this attentiveness to language. Secondly, learning about the dimensions, and complexity, of constitutional life requires a disposition of *humility*. We must recognise that any kind of constitutional

---

9 Ibid.

understanding we develop, or attempt to construct, will always be partial and finite compared with the rich complexity of the actuality of constitutional life. *Humility*, however, is intended to be different from a scepticism that can easily become a sense of futility in understanding. The sobriety of *humility* is not without its hope in the acknowledgement that conceptual schemes and procedures are partial and that new horizons of meaning are always possible. Ultimately this playful sense of the possible becomes, in turn, recognition of that possibility of renewal of our common traditions of understanding. Finally, learning constitutional life implies the serious sense of common commitments in relation to others; constitutional life is a burden of *mutuality* whereby we recognise each other as disclosures of the meaning of constitutional commitments. Each judgement or effort to interpret our constitutional life takes us back to the *mutuality* implied in our language.

It is worth reiterating that the foregoing considerations of transformation, humility and mutuality are not intended to be prescriptions about how we learn about our constitutional life. Furthermore, they are not intended to be ethical considerations by which action can be judged as exemplary or falling short. Instead what we are seeking are possible dispositions towards an approach to learning about our constitutional life that are distinct from the way in which we acquire and dispose of knowledge as a technique and with the sense that knowledge and thinking (about constitutions) cannot be wholly construed instrumentally.

Such an attempt to place the way in which we come to know, or recognise, the commitments of a constitutional life within the effort to consider afresh what it is we mean by 'learning' brings us back to consider something fundamental about hermeneutics itself – the 'method' which has guided the thinking about constitutionalism throughout this book. In the Platonic dialogue *Protagoras* it was a messenger figure, Hermes, who communicated the message of justice between Gods and mortals in order to make the civic life possible, thus overcoming the radical alienation between humans and their environment. Finally, with our discussion about learning, it might be possible to see this 'myth' in a new light which confronts the way in which we now think about our civic life. At the heart of the 'myth' is the notion of a 'message'. Indeed, it is from the very sense of a 'message' that the word Hermeneutics arises – the message is conveyed by Hermes, from another place. The action of Hermes is a movement to *convey* the message, but what is the action of those mortals who dwell on earth? Can it be said that it is not an action at all but rather a 'waiting' for a message and a patience to be able to 'hear' such a message when it arrives? If this is how we understand the relevance of this myth then the essence of hermeneutics, as a form of learning, would seem to involve a kind of *restfulness* whereby we wait for a message as opposed to setting ourselves upon the task of striving or working to find it out. It is in the quiet of *restfulness* that it might be possible to hear something of the message about the justice of civic life. Surely the groping for words and ways of conveying this idea of the learning of hermeneutics as *restfulness* suggest how unfamiliar we are with this way of learning and how difficult it is. As enigmatic as these sketches seem to be they do point us towards a direction in which we can perhaps appreciate the deeper connections between hermeneutics and constitutional life and follow a path to learning about them. There can be no doubt that there is much further reflection to be done, but this, perhaps, can be conducted in the spirit of waiting for what might appear at first to be 'strange' as opposed to working on what is already familiar.

Finally, in respect of this relationship between hermeneutics and constitutional life that we have been exploring through 'learning' it is also possible to return, or recall, the other important theme of this book – that is, the problematical issue of security as a constitutional public good. In Chapter 4 the position of security as an ambivalent public good was considered, in particular, in the work of Loader and Walker. Security was thought about as an important example of how it could connect to conditions of political trust and solidarity rather than being inimical to them. It is both interesting and suggestive that in a passage concerning the direction towards what the authors' term 'axiomatic security' they come to emphasise the crucial connection between living securely with risk and 'learning' or 'education':

> ...security is a necessary platform *for* any kind of political society, irrespective of the range of other goods that it chooses to value and pursue. But it is to argue, further, that security is an education *in* society. Security concerns educate, they teach people how to be with each other, they offer a daily tutorial in the rudiments of being social.[10]

From the recognition that security it is essential to understand the nature or essence of political trust and community we get the acknowledgement that this involves a connection with the activity of learning, specifically the task of learning to live with risk. However, we might ask what kind of 'education in society' does security teach us, or alternatively, how do we learn about political trust from recognising the preconditions of security? The answer that the authors' provide is clearly stated in a later passage:

> It is security understood and re-configured not as a form of perpetual *striving*, but as a state of well *being* – a state in which we are able to live – and live together – securely with risk.[11]

The words that the authors' have emphasised in this passage seem to be highly significant; they imply that wellbeing, as an aspect of living or how we are living, can only be recognised once we relinquish or release ourselves from a perpetual *striving* for security. Learning, or what we learn about, seems to be to give a release from perpetual *striving*. How does learning achieve this? It would seem that to answer this question we would need to understand what might be implied by *striving for security*.

10 Loader and Walker, *Civilising Security*, p. 167.

11 Ibid., p. 169. Authors' emphasis.

Striving for security recalls the idea of 'governmentality' and the techniques of the apparatus of security that we explored through the writings of Michel Foucault. In this sense, striving becomes equated with an instrumentality which comes to dominate, as a form of rationality, and obscures those features of the good which are constitutional. In thinking about the relationship between security and constitutionalism we must take seriously what is at stake in the contrast presented by Loader and Walker between a *striving* for security and the path towards 'well-*being*'. For if 'wellbeing' is considered to be the answer to *striving* it must also indicate its counter-word: *restfulness*. It is in the circumstances that security has become predominant that we can hear its counter-word, *restfulness*, and in echoing the message of hermeneutics we can perhaps begin to think about the basis of political trust that resides in the good of 'security'.[12]

Epilogue

In 1819 the Huguenot Swiss-French thinker, and politician, Benjamin Constant delivered a lecture at the *Athénée Royal* in which he propounds the difference between 'ancient' and 'modern' freedoms and the different political structures under which such liberties become possible.[13] Constant directs his audience to consider what they might mean when they think of the liberty of their own age – the early nineteenth century – and suggests that this is very different to the liberty of antiquity. He proffers this view to his contemporaries assembled at the *Athénée Royal*:

> Finally it is everyone's right to exercise some influence on the administration of the government, either by electing all or particular officials, or through

12 In arriving at this interpretation of those passages quoted from Loader and Walker I have been influenced by the following dialogue from Martin Heidegger, 'A Triadic Conversation', *Country Path Conversations* (translated by Bret W. Davis, Bloomington, IN: Indiana University Press, 2010).

'SCHOLAR: ... the growing appreciation of achievement and work is necessarily accompanied by increased work on securing the possibilities and expansion of achievement.

SCIENTIST: Which is indeed also why the idea of a new world order, that is, the distribution of opportunities, means and goals for work – just like the idea of a world security, that is, of a securing of the accomplishment of work and its conditions – is attaining an increasingly clear configuration.

GUIDE: But presumably security [*Sicherheit*] does not all come from efforts at securing [*Sicherungen*], which can only drive their own pre-requisite, namely insecurity, forth in increased degrees. Security rests [*berucht*] solely in restful repose [*Ruhe*], because through this it is reduced to insignificant concern', at p. 45.

13 Originally published in the collection, *Collection Complète des Ouvrages Publiés sur le Gouvernement Représentif et la Constitution Actuelle de la France, ou Cours de Politique Constitutionelle* (Paris and Rouen, 1820), Vol. 4, pp. 238–274.

> representations, petitions, demands to which the authorities are more or less compelled to pay heed. Now compare this liberty with that of the ancients.[14]

The liberty of the ancients, for Constant, consisted of what he describes as a 'complete subjection of the individual to the authority of the community'.[15] Constant emphasises that as a participant in public affairs, the individual (in so far as *he* was able to participate) had considerable liberty, he had no notion of private rights at all: 'men were, so to speak, merely machines, whose gears and cog-wheels were regulated by the law'.[16] In particular, the kind of private activity that Constant seeks to emphasise and advance as the most worthy is that of trade or commerce.[17] The importance and the growth of trade and commerce, seen as a civilising endeavour,[18] had become particularly prominent in the century preceding Constant, and he not only argues that this was very different from the sort of commerce and trade of the ancient world, but he also contends that this rests on the system of modern liberty.[19]

> Let power therefore resign itself: we must have liberty and we shall have it. But since the liberty we need is different from that of the ancients, it needs a different organization from the one which would suit ancient liberty.[20]

It might have seemed very clear to Constant's listeners that they were indeed to enjoy the processes of history playing itself out in the coalescing of freedom around the notion of private liberty, supported by the economy of goods and services, and guaranteed by the state as the institutional form that underpins this liberty. Very nearly two hundred years later we might listen to this lecture and still remain convinced that, on the whole, this characterisation of modern freedom is correct

---

14 Benjamin Constant, 'The Liberty of the Ancients Compared with that of the Moderns', in *Cambridge Texts in the History of Political Thought: Constant Political Writings*, edited by Biancamaria Fontana (Cambridge: Cambridge University Press, 1988) at p. 311.

15 Ibid.

16 Ibid., p. 312.

17 Ibid., p. 315, pp. 324–325. Perhaps, here he is demonstrating his intellectual debts to the thinkers of the Scottish Enlightenment in particular and also John Locke. It is acknowledged that Constant was influenced by British scholarship and he studied in Scotland.

18 For instance, note the passage in which Constant claims, 'Commerce has brought nations closer, it has given them customs and habits which are almost identical; the heads of states may be enemies: the peoples are compatriots', Ibid., p. 325.

19 Ibid., p. 315, 'commerce inspires in men a vivid love of individual independence. Commerce supplies their needs and satisfies their desires, without the intervention of the authorities'.

20 Ibid., p. 325.

and that it is only a question of time for the 'end of history' to play itself out.[21] Without necessarily sharing the notion that history is marked by some of kind of meaningful progress towards a homogenous and universal form of freedom and politics, it is possible to appreciate the ingenuity of Constant's construction of the 'progression' of politics and freedom from the ancient world to that of the modern.

It is a peculiarity of the EU that it seems to sit uneasily in this narrative of the progress of history; on the one hand it might be viewed as the first attempts at the completion, or extension, of the liberal and enlightenment traditions of the state; or, on the other hand, it might be considered as a new episode in the administration of government and freedom. To some extent I think this issue strikes at the culture of uncertainty and institutional examination that occurs in society at large and also in academia surrounding the 'post-state constellation' of the EU. This book has not sought to confront or even critique this issue directly. In part this was because of the desire to avoid being understood as attempting to uncover a justification for the EU, or alternatively to arbitrarily indicate its limits, either inherently or by relation to the state. Equally, such a stance was necessitated by the sense that the *concept* of the 'state' had itself become a way of avoiding thinking about the complicated practices developing in the EU. The constitutional analysis has instead proceeded from the basis that, taking the example of the AFSJ, it is possible to understand that the technical delivery of internal security needs (which are different from the instrumental needs of internal security) inevitably runs up against concerns as to the constitutional legitimacy of that which is taking place, but that such concerns will not be displaced by appealing to the 'concept' of the state. The practices of governing taking place in the AFSJ, and the EU, must be engaged with as constitutional practices and, therefore, require us to take seriously the claim that freedom, security and justice are constitutional commitments of the EU; otherwise, the area of freedom, security and justice may risk becoming precisely the representation of the unquenchable appetite for the instrumental delivery of security. Primarily, therefore, taking the EU as a site for constitutional practice is a call to preserve and to find possible ways of acknowledging constitutional life.

21 Represented in the writing of Francis Fukuyama, *The End of History and the Last Man* (New York: Maxwell Macmillan, 1992) and the writings of Alexandre Kojève, *Outline of a Phenomenology of Right*, translated and edited by Bryan-Paul Frost (Lanham, MD: Rowman and Littlefield, 2000).

Bibliography

Agamben, Giorgio. *State of Exception*, translated by Kevin Attell (Chicago: University of Chicago Press, 2005).

Anderson, Malcolm. Den Boer, Monica. Cullen, Peter. Gilmore, William C., Raab, Charles D. and Walker, Neil. *Policing in the European Union* (Oxford: Clarendon Press, 1995).

Arendt, Hannah. *Between Past and Future: Eight Exercises in Political Thought* (New York: Penguin Classics, 1978).

Arendt, Hannah. *On Revolution* (London: Penguin Books, 1990).

Arendt, Hannah. *The Human Condition* (Chicago, IL: University of Chicago Press, 1998).

Aristotle. *Nicomachean Ethics of Aristotle*, translated by Sir David Ross (London: Oxford University Press, 1954).

Avbelj, Matej and Komárek, Jan. 'Four Visions of Constitutional Pluralism', 4 *European Constitutional Law Review* (2008), pp. 524–527.

Bankowski, Zenon and Christodoulidis, Emilios. 'The European Union as an Essentially Contested Project', in *The European Union and its Order: The Legal Theory of European Integration*, edited by Zenon Bankowski and Andrew Scott (Oxford: Blackwell, 1999).

Beck, Ulrich, Giddens, Anthony and Lash, Scott. *Reflexive Modernization: Politics, Tradition and Aesthetics in the Modern Social Order* (Cambridge: Polity Press, 1994).

Beck, Ulrich. *Risk Society: Towards a New Modernity* (London: Sage, 1992).

Bigo, Didier. 'Liberty, whose Liberty? The Hague Programme and the Conception of Freedom' in *Security Versus Freedom: A Challenge for Europe's Future*, edited by Thierry Balzacq and Sergio Carrera (Aldershot: Ashgate, 2006).

Brouwer, Evelien. 'Data Surveillance and Border Control in the EU', in *Security Versus Freedom: A Challenge for Europe's Future*, edited by Thierry Balzacq and Sergio Carrera (Aldershot: Ashgate, 2006).

Buzan, Barry. *People, States and Fear: An Agenda for International Security Studies in the Post-Cold War Era* (London: Harvester Wheatsheaf, 1991).

Buzan, Barry, Wæver, Ole and de Wilde, Japp. *Security: A New Framework for Analysis* (Boulder CO: Lynne Rienner, 1998).

Collingwood, Robin G. *The Idea of History* (Oxford: Oxford University Press, 1994).

Constant, Benjamin. 'The Liberty of the Ancients Compared with that of the Moderns', in *Cambridge Texts in the History of Political Thought: Constant*

Political Writings, edited by Biancamaria Fontana (Cambridge: Cambridge University Press, 1988).

Craig, Paul. 'Constitutions, Constitutionalism and the European Union', 7 *European Law Journal* (2001), pp. 125–150.

Croce, Benedetto. *Teoria e Storia della Storiografia* (Bari: Laterza, 1973).

de Saussure, Ferdinand. *Cours de Linguistique Générale* (Paris: Payot, 1985).

Dean, Mitchell. *Governmentality: Power and Rule in Modern Society* (London: Sage, 2010).

den Boer, Monica. 'Europe and the Art of International Police Co-operation: Free Fall or Measured Scenario?' in *Legal Issues of the Maastricht Treaty*, edited by David O'Keeffe and Patrick Twomey (London: Chancery Law Publishers, 1994).

Dougan, Michael. 'Minimum Harmonization and the Internal Market', 37 *Common Market Law Review* (2000), pp. 853–885.

Douglas-Scott, Sionaidh 'The Rule of Law in the European Union – Putting the Security into the Area of Freedom, Security and Justice', 29 *European Law Review* (2004), pp. 219–242.

Duff, Andrew. *The Struggle for Europe's Constitution* (London: Federal Trust, 2005).

Elster, Jon. *Ulysses Unbound; Studies in Rationality, Pre-commitments and Constraints* (Cambridge: Cambridge University Press, 2000).

Fletcher, Maria. 'Schengen, the European Court of Justice and Flexibility under the Lisbon Treaty: Balancing the UK's "Ins" and "Outs"', 5 *European Constitutional Law Review* (2009), pp. 71–98.

Foqué, René. 'Criminal Justice in a Democracy: Towards a Relational Conception of Criminal Law and Punishment', 2 *Criminal Law and Philosophy* (2008), pp. 207–227.

Foucault, Michel. *Discipline and Punish: The Birth of the Prison* (London: Penguin Books, 1991).

Foucault, Michel. *Security, Territory, Population* (London: Palgrave Macmillan, 2004).

Foucault, Michel. *The Hermeneutics of the Subject* (New York: Picador, 2004).

Frohlich, Norman, Oppenheimer, Joe and Young, Oran. *Political Leadership and Collective Goods* (Princeton, NJ: Princeton University Press, 1971).

Fukuyama, Francis. *The End of History and the Last Man* (New York: Maxwell Macmillan, 1992).

Gadamer, Hans-Georg. 'The Universality of the Hermeneutical Problem', in *Philosophical Hermeneutics*, translated and edited by David Linge (Berkeley, CA: University of California Press, 1977).

Gadamer, Hans-Georg. *Truth and Method*, translated by Joel Weinsheimer (London: Continuum Press, 2004).

Gibbs, Alun. 'Reasoned Balance in Europe's Area of Freedom, Security and Justice', 17 *European Law Journal*, pp. 121–137.

Gibbs, Nathan. 'European Constitutionalism, the Temporal Dimension of Juridical Order and Modern Social Imaginary', 21 *Law and Critique* (2010), pp. 147–162.

Giddens, Anthony. *The Constitution of Society: An Outline of a Theory of Structuration* (Cambridge: Polity Press, 1984).

Grimm, Dieter. 'Integration by Constitution' 3 *ICON* (2005), pp. 193–208.

Guild, Elspeth. 'The Bitter Fruits of a Common Asylum Policy', in *Security Versus Freedom: A Challenge for Europe's Future*, edited by Thierry Balzacq and Sergio Carrera (Aldershot: Ashgate, 2006).

Günther, Klaus. 'World Citizens between Freedom and Security', 12(3) *Constellations* (2005), pp. 379–391.

Habermas, Jürgen. 'Why Europe Needs a Constitution', 11 *New Left Review* (2001), pp. 5–26.

Habermas, Jürgen. *The Postnational Constellation: Political Essays*, translated and edited by Max Pensky (Cambridge, MA: MIT Press, 2001).

Haltern, Ulrich. 'Pathos and Patina: The Failure and Promise of Constitutionalism in the European Imagination', 9 *European Law Journal* (2003), pp. 14–44.

Hartley, Trevor. *Constitutional Problems of the European Union* (Oxford: Hart Publishing, 1999).

Heidegger, Martin. *Being and Time*, translated by John Macquarrie and Edward Robinson (Oxford, Blackwells, 1962).

Heidegger, Martin. *Ontology: The Hermeneutics of Facticity*, translated by John van Buren (Bloomington, IN: Indiana University Press, 1999).

Heidegger, Martin. 'A Triadic Conversation', *Country Path Conversations*, translated by Bret W. Davis (Bloomington, IN: Indiana University Press, 2010).

Heidegger, Martin. *Basic Writings*, edited by David Farrell Krell (London: Routledge, 2010).

Kojève, Alexandre. *Outline of a Phenomenology of Right*, translated and edited by Bryan-Paul Frost (Lanham, MD: Rowman and Littlefield, 2000).

Kostakopoulou, Theodora. *Citizenship, Identity and Immigration in the European Union: Between Past and Future* (Manchester: Manchester University Press, 2001).

Kostakopolou, Theodora. 'The Area of Freedom, Security and Justice under the New Constitution', *Academy of European Law*, European University Institute, July 2005.

Kumm, Mattias. 'The Jurisprudence of Constitutional Conflict: Constitutional Supremacy in Europe before and after the Constitutional Treaty', 11 *European Law Journal* (2005), pp. 262–307.

Landau, Martin. *Political Theory and Political Science: Studies in the Methodology of Political Inquiry* (New Jersey: Humanities Press, 1979).

Levi, Michael and Wall, David. 'Technologies, Security, and Privacy in the Post-9/11 European Information Society', 31 *Journal of Law and Society* (2004), pp. 194–220.

Lindahl, Hans (ed.). *A Right to Inclusion and Exclusion: Normative Fault-lines of the EU's Area of Freedom, Security and Justice* (Oxford: Hart Publishing, 2009).

Lindahl, Hans. 'European Integration: Popular Sovereignty and a Politics of Boundaries', 6 *European Law Journal* (2000), pp. 239–256.

Lindahl, Hans. 'Finding a Place for Freedom, Security and Justice: The European Union's Claim to Territorial Unity', 29 *European Law Review* (2004), pp. 461–484.

Lloyd-Jones, Hugh. *The Justice of Zeus* (Berkeley, CA: University of California Press, 1971).

Loader, Ian and Neil Walker. *Civilizing Security* (Cambridge: Cambridge University Press, 2007).

Lodge, Juliet. 'Transparency, Justice and Territoriality: The EU Border Challenge' in *Security Versus Freedom: A Challenge for Europe's Future*, edited by Thierry Balzacq and Sergio Carrera (Aldershot: Ashgate, 2006).

Lord, Christopher and Magnette, Paul. 'E Pluribus Unum? Creative Disagreement about Legitimacy in the EU', 42 *JCMS* (2004), pp. 183–202.

MacCormick, Neil. *Questioning Sovereignty: Law, State and Nation in the European Commonwealth* (Oxford: Oxford University Press, 1999).

Mancini, Giovanni. 'Europe: The Case for Statehood', 4 *European Law Journal* (1998), pp. 43–62.

McCormick, John. *Carl Schmitt's Critique of Liberalism: Against Politics as Technology* (Cambridge: Cambridge University Press, 1997).

Michelman, Frank. 'Constitutional Authorship', in *Constitutionalism: Philosophical Foundations*, edited by Larry Alexander (Cambridge: Cambridge University Press 1998).

Mitsilegas, Valsamis. 'The Borders Paradox: The Surveillance of Movement in a Union without Internal Frontiers', in *A Right to Inclusion and Exclusion: Normative Fault-lines of the EU's Area of Freedom, Security and Justice*, edited by Hans Lindahl (Oxford: Hart Publishing, 2009).

Mitsilegas, Valsamis. 'The Transformation of Criminal Law in the Area of Freedom, Security and Justice', 26 *Yearbook of European Law* (2007), pp. 1–32.

Monar, Jorg. 'Justice and Home Affairs in the Treaty of Amsterdam: Reform at the Price of Fragmentation', 23 *European Law Review* (1998), pp. 320–335.

Nuotio, Kimmo. 'On the Significance of Criminal Justice for a Europe "United in Diversity"', in *Europe in Search of Meaning and Purpose*, edited by Kimmo Nuotio (Helsinki: University of Helsinki Publications, 2004).

O'Keeffe, David. 'Reforming the Third Pillar: Transparency and Structural Reform in the Long-Term Perspective', in *Justice and Home Affairs in the EU: The Development of the Third Pillar*, edited by Roland Bieber and Jorg Monar (European University Press, Bruges Conference, 1995).

Oakeshott, Michael. 'Political Education', in *Rationalism in Politics and Other Essays* (Indianapolis, IN: Liberty Fund, 1991).

Oakeshott, Michael. *On Human Conduct* (Oxford: Clarendon Press, 1990).
Oakeshott, Michael. *Lectures in the History of Political Thought*, edited by Terry Nardin and Luke O'Sullivan (Exeter: Imprint Academic, 2006).
Olsen, Mancur. *A Theory of Groups and Organizations* (Cambridge, MA: Harvard University Press, 1965).
Orwell, George. *Nineteen Eighty-Four* (London: Penguin Books, 1954).
Peers, Steve. *Justice and Home Affairs* (Oxford: Oxford University Press, 2006).
Perry, Michael J. 'What Is "the Constitution"?', in *Constitutionalism: Philosophical Foundations*, edited by Larry Alexander (Cambridge: Cambridge University Press 1998).
Raz, Joseph. 'Right Based Moralities', in *Theories of Rights*, edited by Jeremy Waldron (Oxford: Oxford University Press, 1984).
Réaume, Denise. 'Individuals, Groups, and Rights to Public Goods', 38 *The University of Toronto Law Journal* (1988), pp. 1–27.
Richards, David. *Foundations of American Constitutionalism* (Oxford: Oxford University Press, 1989).
Schilling, Theodor. 'The Autonomy of the Community Legal Order: An Analysis of Possible Foundations', 37 *Harvard International Law Journal* (1996), pp. 389–409.
Schmitt, Carl. *Political Theology: Four Chapters on the Concept of Sovereignty*, translated by George Schwab (Cambridge, MA, MIT Press, 1985).
Siedentop, Larry. *Democracy in Europe* (London: Allen Lane, 2000).
Taylor, Charles. *Human Agency and Language: Philosophical Papers Volume 1* (Cambridge: Cambridge University Press, 1985).
Taylor, Charles. *Sources of the Self: The Making of the Modern Identity* (Cambridge: Cambridge University Press, 1989).
Taylor, Charles. *Philosophical Arguments* (Cambridge, MA: Harvard University Press, 1997).
Taylor, Charles. *The Secular Age* (London: The Belknap Press of Harvard University, 2007).
Tully, Jim. *Strange Multiplicity: Constitutionalism in an Age of Diversity* (Cambridge: Cambridge University Press, 1995).
Twomey, Patrick. 'Constructing a Secure Space: The Area of Freedom, Security and Justice', in *Legal Issues of the Amsterdam Treaty*, edited by David O'Keeffe and Patrick Twomey (Oxford: Hart Publishing, 1999).
Ullmann, Walter. *A History of Political Thought in the Middle Ages* (Harmondsworth: Penguin Books, 1965).
van der Mei, Peter. *Free Movement of Persons within the European Community: Cross Border Access to Public Benefits* (Oxford: Hart Publishing, 2003).
Von Bogdandy, Armin. 'The European Union as a Human Rights Organization? Human Rights at the Core of the European Union', 37 *Common Market Law Review* (2000), pp. 1307–1338.
Wæver, Ole, Buzan, Barry, Kelstrup, Morten and Lemaitre, Pierre. *Identity, Migration and the New Security Agenda in Europe* (London: Pinter, 1993).

Walker, Neil and Loughlin, Martin (eds). *The Paradox of Constitutionalism: Constituent Power and Constitutional Form* (Oxford: Oxford University Press, 2007).

Walker, Neil. 'Europe's Constitutional Momentum and the Search for Polity Legitimacy', 3 *I.CON* (2005), pp. 201–238.

Walker, Neil. 'In Search of the Area of Freedom, Security and Justice: A Constitutional Odyssey', in *Europe's Area of Freedom, Security and Justice,* edited by Neil Walker (Oxford: Oxford University Press, 2004).

Ward, Ian. 'Beyond Constitutionalism: the Search for the European Political Imagination', 7 *European Law Journal* (2001), pp. 32–40.

Weiler, Joseph H.H. and Haltern, Ulrich. 'The Autonomy of the Community Legal Order – Through the Looking Glass', 37 *Harvard International Law Journal* (1996), pp. 411–448.

Weiler, Joseph H.H. 'Does Europe Need a Constitution? Reflections on Demos, Telos and the German Maastricht Decision', 1 *European Law Journal* (1995), pp. 219–258.

Weiler, Joseph H.H. 'Europe's Tragic Choice', Contribution to the Symposium: Responses to Joschka Fischer, *Jean Monnet Working Papers* 7/00 (2000), New York: NYU School of Law.

Weiler, Joseph H.H. *The Constitution of Europe: Do the New Clothes have a New Emperor?* (Cambridge: Cambridge University Press, 1999).

Williams, Michael C. 'Words, Images, Enemies: Securitization and International Politics', 47 *International Studies Quarterly* (2003), pp. 511–531.

Wolin, Sheldon. *Politics and Vision: Continuity and Innovation in Western Political Thought* (Boston: Little Brown, 1960).

Zedner, Lucia. *Security* (London: Routledge, 2009).

Zedner, Lucia. 'Too much Security?' 31 *International Journal of the Sociology of Law* (2003), pp. 155–184.

Zedner, Lucia. *Technologies of Insecurity: Surveillance and Security of Everyday Life* (London: Routledge, 2008).

Index

www.ingramcontent.com/pod-product-compliance
Ingram Content Group UK Ltd.
Pitfield, Milton Keynes, MK11 3LW, UK
UKHW011018180926
475701UK00004B/804
* 9 7 8 1 1 3 8 2 5 6 7 6 7 *